J. Hudson Taylor

A Retrospect

Thou shalt remember all the way which the Lord thy God led thee.

A Retrospect

The Story Behind My Zeal for Missions

J. Hudson Taylor

ANEKO
PRESS

Reprint edition
A Retrospect – J. Hudson Taylor
Copyright © 2015
First edition published 1894

Cover Design: Amber Burger
Cover Photography: caramelina/Shutterstock
Editors: Sheila Wilkinson, Ruth Zetek

Printed in the United States of America
Aneko Press – *Our Readers Matter*™
www.anekopress.com
Aneko Press, Life Sentence Publishing, and our logos are trademarks of
Life Sentence Publishing, Inc.
203 E. Birch Street
P.O. Box 652
Abbotsford, WI 54405

BIOGRAPHY & AUTOBIOGRAPHY / Religious

Paperback ISBN: 978-1-62245-200-2
eBook ISBN: 978-1-62245-220-0
10 9 8 7 6 5 4 3 2 1
Available where books are sold.
Share this book on Facebook:

Contents

The "Lammermuir" Party, see Chapter 19

CHAPTER 1

The Power of Prayer

The following account of some of the experiences that led to the formation of the China Inland Mission and the form it developed first appeared in the pages of *China's Millions*. Many who read it asked that it might appear in a separate form. Miss Guinness incorporated it in the *Story Of The China Inland Mission*, a record which contained the account of God's goodness to the beginning of 1894. But this edition is brought out for friends still asking for it in pamphlet form for wider distribution.

Much of the material was taken from notes of addresses given in China during a conference of our missionaries. This will account for the direct and narrative form of the papers, which I thought was not necessary to change.

It is always helpful to us to fix our attention on the God-ward aspect of Christian work – to realize that the work of God does not mean so much man's work for God as God's own work through man. Furthermore, in our privileged position of fellow workers with Him, while recognizing all the benefits and blessings to be bestowed on a sin-stricken world through the proclamation of the gospel and the spread of the truth, we should never lose sight of the higher aspect of our work. The higher goal involves obedience to God, bringing glory to His name, and gladdening the heart of our God and Father by living and serving as His beloved children.

Many circumstances in my own early life and service presented this aspect of work vividly to me. As I think of some of them, I am reminded of how much the cause of missions is indebted to many who are never permitted to see the mission field themselves. It may be that many who are unable to give of their substance will be surprised in the Great Day to see how much the work has been advanced by their love, their sympathy, and their prayers.

For me and the work that I have been permitted to do for God, I owe an unspeakable debt of gratitude to my beloved and honored parents. They have passed away and entered into rest, but the influence of their lives will never pass away.

Many years ago, probably about 1830, the heart of my dear father was deeply stirred about the spiritual state of China. He had read several books, particularly an account of the travels of Captain Basil Hall. Though he was an earnest and successful evangelist at home, his circumstances were such as to prevent him from ever going to China for personal service. But he was led to pray that if God should give him a son, he might be called and privileged to labor in the vast, needy empire, which was then sealed against the truth. I was not aware of this desire or prayer until my return to England, more than seven years after I had sailed for China. It was very interesting to learn how prayer offered before my birth had been answered in this matter.

All thought of my becoming a missionary was abandoned for many years by my dear parents because of the feebleness of my health. When the time came, however, God gave increased health, and my life has been spared. Strength has been given for toilsome service both in the mission field and at home, while many stronger men and women have succumbed.

I had many opportunities in early years to learn the value of prayer and the Word of God. It delighted my dear parents to point out that if there were any such being as God, to trust Him, to obey Him, and to be fully given to His service must be the best and wisest course for both others and me. But in spite of these helpful examples and precepts, my heart was unchanged. Often I had tried to make myself a Christian. When I failed in such efforts, I began to think that for some reason or other I could not be saved. I thought that the best I could do was to take my fill of this world, as there was no hope for me beyond the grave.

While in this state of mind, I met people who held skeptical and infidel views, and I accepted their teaching. I was only too thankful for some hope of escape from the doom which, if my parents were right and the Bible true, awaited the impenitent. It may seem strange to say it, but I have often felt thankful for the experience of this time of skepticism. The inconsistencies of Christian people, who professed to believe their Bibles but were content to live as if there were no such book, had been one of the strongest arguments of my skeptical companions. I frequently felt and said that if I pretended to believe the Bible, I would at least attempt to live by it. I would put it to the test, and if it failed to be true and reliable, I would throw it overboard altogether. I retained these views when the Lord was pleased to bring me to Himself; I think I may say that since then, I have put God's Word to the test. Certainly, it has never failed me. I have never had reason to regret the confidence I have placed in its promises or to lament following the guidance I have found in its directions.

Let me tell you how God answered the prayers of my dear mother and my beloved sister (now Mrs. Broomhall), for my conversion. On a day which I shall never forget, when I was about fifteen years old, my dear mother was away from home. I decided to have a holiday; in the afternoon, I looked through my father's library to find a book with which to while away the unoccupied hours. Nothing attracting me, I turned over a little basket of pamphlets and selected a gospel tract that looked interesting. I said to myself, "There will be a story at the beginning and a sermon or moral at the close. I will take the former and leave the latter for those who like it."

I sat down to read the little book in an utterly unconcerned state of mind, believing that if there were any salvation, it was not for me. My distinct intention was to put the tract away as soon as it should seem tedious. I may say that it was not uncommon in those days to call conversion "becoming serious." Judging by the faces of some of its professors, it appeared to be a very serious matter indeed. Would it not be well if the people of God had always telltale faces, evincing the blessings and gladness of salvation so clearly that unconverted people might have to call conversion "becoming joyful" instead of "becoming serious"?

Little did I know at the time what was going on in the heart of my dear mother, seventy or eighty miles away. She rose from the dinner table that afternoon with an intense yearning for the conversion of her boy. Being absent from home, she had more leisure than she could otherwise secure; this afforded her a special opportunity of pleading with God on my behalf. She went to her room, turned the key in the door, and resolved not to leave that spot until her prayers were answered. Hour after hour did that dear mother plead for me, until at length she could pray no longer. She was constrained to praise God for that which His Spirit taught her had already been accomplished – the conversion of her only son.

In the meantime, I had taken up this little tract. While reading it, I was struck with the phrase "The finished work of Christ." The thought passed through my mind: "Why does the author use this expression? Why not say 'the atoning or propitiatory work of Christ'?" Immediately the words *It is finished* suggested themselves to my mind. What was finished? And I at once replied, "A full and perfect atonement and satisfaction for sin: the debt was paid by the Substitute; Christ died for our sins, and not for ours only, but also for the sins of the whole world." Then came the thought: "If the whole work was finished and the whole debt paid, what is there left for me to do?" And with this, as light flashed into my soul by the Holy Spirit, joyful conviction dawned on me that there was nothing in the world to be done but to fall down on my knees, accept this Savior and His salvation, and praise Him forevermore. Thus, while my dear mother was praising God on her knees in her chamber, I was praising Him in the old warehouse where I had gone to read this little book at my leisure.

Several days elapsed before I ventured to make my beloved sister the confidante of my joy, and then only after she had promised not to tell anyone of my soul secret. When our dear mother came home two weeks later, I was the first to meet her at the door and tell her I had such glad news to give. I can almost feel that dear mother's arms around my neck, as she pressed me to her bosom and said, "I know, my boy; I have been rejoicing for two weeks in the glad tidings you have to tell me."

"Why," I asked in surprise, "has Amelia broken her promise? She said she would tell no one." My dear mother assured me that it was not from any human source that she had learned the news, and went on to tell the little incident mentioned above. You will agree with me that it would be strange, indeed, if I were not a believer in the power of prayer.

Nor was this all. Soon after, I picked up a pocket book exactly like one of my own. Thinking that it was mine, I opened it. The lines that caught my eye were an entry in the little diary, which belonged to my sister, indicating that she would give herself daily to prayer until God should answer in the conversion of her brother. Exactly one month later, the Lord was pleased to turn me from darkness to light.

Being brought up in such a circle and saved under such circumstances had a natural effect on my view of prayer from the commencement of my Christian life. I was led to feel that the promises were very real and prayer was a sober matter-of-fact transacting of business with God, whether on my own behalf or on behalf of those for whom I sought His blessing.

CHAPTER 2

The Call to Service

The first joys of conversion passed away after a time and grew into a period of painful deadness of soul with much conflict. But this also ended, leaving a deepened sense of personal weakness and dependence on the Lord as the only keeper, as well as Savior of His people. How sweet to the soul, wearied and disappointed in its struggles with sin, is the calm repose of trust in the shepherd of Israel.

During a leisurely afternoon not many months after my conversion, I retired to my room to spend time in communion with God. Well do I remember that occasion. In the gladness of my heart, I poured out my soul before God. Again and again I confessed my grateful love to Him who had done everything for me. He had saved me when I had given up all hope and even desire for salvation. I begged Him to give me some work to do for Him, as an outlet for love and gratitude. I asked for some self-denying service, no matter what it might be, however trying or however trivial. I prayed for something with which He would be pleased that I might do for Him who had done so much for me. I remember how I put myself, my life, my friends, and my all upon the altar in unreserved consecration. I recall the deep solemnity that came over my soul with the assurance that my offering was accepted. The presence of God became unutterably real and blessed; and though but a child under sixteen, I remember stretching myself on the ground and lying there silent before Him with unspeakable awe and joy.

I did not know for what service I had been accepted, but a

deep consciousness that I was no longer my own took possession of me, which has never since been rescinded. It has been a very practical consciousness. Two or three years later, propositions of an unusually favorable nature were made to me with regard to medical study, on the condition of my becoming apprenticed to the medical man who was my friend and teacher. But I felt I dared not accept any binding engagement such as was suggested. I was not my own to give myself away, for I knew not when or how He might call me for service. I was His alone, and I felt I must keep myself free for His disposal.

Within a few months of this time of consecration, the Lord impressed upon my soul that it was in China that He wanted me. It seemed to me highly probable that the work to which I was thus called might cost me my life, for China was not then open as it is now. But few missionary societies had workers in China at that time, and only a few books on the subject of China missions were accessible to me. I learned, however, that the Congregational minister of my native town possessed a copy of Walter Henry Medhurst's book *China: Its State and Prospects*, and I called upon him to loan the book to me. He kindly granted my request, asking me why I wished to read it. I told him that God had called me to spend my life in missionary service in that land. "And how do you propose to go there?" he inquired. I answered that I did not at all know; it seemed to me probable that I should go as the Twelve and the Seventy had done in Judaea – without purse or scrip, relying on Him who had called me, to supply all my need.

Kindly placing his hand upon my shoulder, the minister replied, "Ah, my boy, as you grow older, you will get wiser than that. Such an idea would do very well in the days when Christ Himself was on earth, but not now."

I have grown older since then, but not wiser. I am more than ever convinced that if we were to take the directions of our Master and the assurances He gave to His first disciples more fully as our guide, we should find them to be as suited to our times as to that time.

Medhurst's book on China emphasized the value of medical missions, and this directed my attention to medical studies as a valuable mode of preparation.

My beloved parents neither discouraged nor encouraged my desire to engage in missionary work. They advised me to use all the means in my power to develop the resources of body, mind, heart, and soul, and to wait prayerfully upon God. They reminded me to follow His guidance should He show me that I was mistaken, or go forward in due time if He should open the way to missionary service. I have often since had occasion to prove the importance of this advice. I began to exercise more in the open air to strengthen my physique. I took my feather bed away and sought to dispense with as many other home comforts as I could to prepare myself for rougher lines of life. I began to do what Christian work was in my power in the way of tract distribution, Sunday school teaching, and visiting the poor and sick, as opportunity afforded.

After a time of preparatory study at home, I went to Hull School of Medicine for medical and surgical training. There I became an assistant to a doctor who was a surgeon to a number of factories. These brought many accident cases to our dispensary and gave me the opportunity of seeing and practicing the minor operations of surgery.

An event took place here that I must not neglect to mention. Before leaving home, my attention was drawn to the subject of setting apart the firstfruits of all one's increase and a proportionate part of one's possessions to the Lord's service. I thought it best to study the question with my Bible in hand before I went away from home and was placed in circumstances which might bias my conclusions by the pressure of surrounding wants and cares. I was thus led to set apart not less than one-tenth of whatever moneys I might earn or become possessed of for the Lord's service. The salary I received as a medical assistant in Hull at that time would have allowed me to do this with ease. But due to changes in the family of my kind friend and employer, it was necessary for me to reside elsewhere. Comfortable quarters were secured with a relative, but I received the exact amount as remuneration for my services that I had to pay for board and lodging.

Now arose in my mind the question: "Ought not this sum also to be tithed?" It was surely a part of my income, and I felt that if it had been a question of government income tax it certainly would not have been excluded. On the other hand, to take a tithe from the whole would not leave me sufficient for other purposes; for some time, I struggled to know what to do. After much thought and prayer, I was led to leave the comfortable quarters and happy circle in which I was now residing and to secure a little lodging in the suburbs – a sitting room and bedroom in one – undertaking to board myself. In this way, I was able to tithe the whole of my income without difficulty. While I felt the change a good deal, it came with no small blessing.

More time was given in my solitude to the study of the Word of God, to visiting the poor, and to evangelistic work on summer evenings than would otherwise have been the case. Brought into contact in this way with many who were in distress, I soon saw the privilege of further economizing and did not find it difficult to give away much more than the proportion of my income I had intended at first.

About this time, a friend drew my attention to the question of the personal and premillennial coming of our Lord Jesus Christ. He gave me a list of passages referring to it, without note or comment, and advised me to ponder the subject. For a while, I gave much time to studying the Scriptures about it, with the result that I was led to see that this same Jesus who left our earth in His resurrection body was to come again. His feet were to stand on the Mount of Olives, and He was to take possession of the temporal throne of His father David, which was promised before His birth. I saw, further, that all through the New Testament the coming of the Lord was the great hope of His people. This was always appealed to as the strongest motive for consecration and service and the greatest comfort in trial and affliction. I learned, too, that the period of His return for His people was not revealed. It was their privilege, from day to day and from hour to hour, to live as men who wait for the Lord. Thus living, it was immaterial whether He should or should not come at any particular hour. The important thing was to be so ready for Him as to be able, whenever He might appear, to give an account of one's stewardship with joy and not with grief.

The effect of this blessed hope was a thoroughly practical one. It led me to look carefully through my little library to see if I had any books that were not needed or likely to be of no further service. I examined my small wardrobe to be quite sure it contained nothing that I should be sorry to give an account of should the Master come at once. The result was that the library was considerably diminished to the benefit of some poor neighbors and to the far greater benefit of my own. I also found I had articles of clothing which might be put to better advantage in other directions.

It has been very helpful to me from time to time through life, as occasion has served, to act again in a similar way. I have never gone through my house from basement to attic, with this object in view, without receiving a great increase of spiritual joy and blessing. I believe we are all in danger of accumulating. It may be from thoughtlessness or from pressure of occupation. Retaining things that would be useful to others, while not needed by ourselves, entails loss of blessing. If all resources of the church of God were utilized well, how much more might be accomplished! How many poor might be fed and naked clothed? And to how many of those, as yet unreached, the gospel might be carried? Let me advise this line of things as a constant habit of mind and a profitable course to be practically adopted whenever circumstances permit.

CHAPTER 3

Preparation for Service

Having now the twofold objective of accustoming myself
to endure hardness and of economizing in order to be
more able to assist those for whom I spent a good deal of time
laboring in the gospel, I soon found that I could live upon much
less than I had previously thought possible. I soon ceased to
use butter, milk, and other such luxuries; I found that by living
mainly on oatmeal and rice with occasional variations, a very
small amount was sufficient for my needs. In this way, I had
more than two-thirds of my income available for other purposes. My experience was that the less I spent on myself and
the more I gave away, the fuller my soul became with happiness
and blessing. Unspeakable joy all day long and every day was
my happy experience. God, even my God, was a living, bright
reality; all I had to do was joyful service.

It was to me a very grave matter, however, to contemplate
going out to China, far away from all human aid, and depend
upon the living God alone for protection, supplies, and help of
every kind. I felt that one's spiritual muscles required strength-
ening for such an undertaking. There was no doubt that if faith
did not fail, God would not fail; but then, what if one's faith
should prove insufficient? I had not at that time learned that
even *If we believe not, yet he abideth faithful: he cannot deny
himself.* It was consequently a very serious question to my mind
– not whether *He* was faithful, but whether I had strong-enough
faith to warrant my embarking on the enterprise set before me.

I thought to myself, "When I get out to China, I shall have

no claim on anyone for anything; my only claim will be on God. How important, therefore, to learn before leaving England to move man through God by prayer alone."

At Hull, my kind employer, who was always busily occupied, wished me to remind him whenever my salary became due. I determined not to do this directly, but to ask that God would bring the fact to his recollection and thus encourage me by answering prayer. At one time, as the day drew near for the payment of a quarter's salary, I was as usual much in prayer about it. The time arrived, but my kind friend made no allusion to the matter. I continued praying. Days passed on, but he did not remember, until at length, on settling up my weekly accounts one Saturday night, I found myself possessed of only a single coin – one half-crown piece. Still I had no lack, and I continued in prayer.

That Sunday was a very happy one. As usual my heart was full and brimming over with blessing. After attending divine service in the morning, my afternoons and evenings were filled with gospel work in the various lodging houses I was accustomed to visit in the lowest part of the town. At such times, it seemed to me as if heaven had begun below, and all that could be looked for was an enlargement of one's capacity for joy, not a truer filling than I possessed. After concluding my last service about ten o'clock that night, a poor man asked me to go and pray with his wife, saying that she was dying. I readily agreed, and on the way to his house, I asked him why he had not sent for the priest, as his accent told me he was an Irishman. He had done so, he said, but the priest refused to come without a payment of eighteen pence, which the man did not possess, because the family was starving. Immediately it occurred to my mind that all the money I had in the world was the solitary half-crown. Moreover, while the basin of water gruel I usually took for supper was awaiting me, and there was sufficient in the house for breakfast in the morning, I certainly had nothing for dinner on the coming day.

Somehow or other there was at once a stoppage in the flow of joy in my heart. Instead of reproving myself, I began to reprove the poor man, telling him that it was very wrong to have allowed matters to get into such a state as he described, and he ought to have applied to the relieving officer. His answer was that he had done so. He was told to come at eleven o'clock the next morning, but he feared that his wife might not live through the night. "Ah," thought I, "if only I had two shillings and a sixpence instead of this half-crown, how gladly would I give these poor people one shilling of it!" But to part with the half-crown was far from my thoughts. I little dreamed that the real truth of the matter was simply that I could trust in God plus one-and-sixpence, but was not yet prepared to trust Him only, without any money at all in my pocket.

My escort led me into a court, down which I followed him with some degree of nervousness. I had found myself there before, and at my last visit I had been very roughly handled, while my tracts were torn to pieces. I had received such a warning not to come again that I felt more than a little concerned. Still, it was the path of duty, and I followed on. Up a miserable flight of stairs into a wretched room, he led me; oh, what a sight presented itself to our eyes! Four or five poor children stood about, their sunken cheeks and temples all telling unmistakably the story of slow starvation. Lying on a wretched pallet was a poor exhausted mother with a tiny infant, thirty-six hours old, moaning rather than crying at her side, for it too seemed spent and failing. "Ah," thought I, "if I had two shillings and a sixpence instead of a half-crown, how gladly should they have one and sixpence of it!" But still a wretched unbelief prevented me from obeying the impulse to relieve their distress at the cost of all I possessed.

It will scarcely seem strange that I was unable to say much to comfort these poor people. I needed comfort myself. I began to tell them, however, that they must not be cast down. Though their circumstances were very distressing, there was a kind and loving Father in heaven. But something within me said, "You hypocrite! Telling these unconverted people about a kind and loving Father in heaven and not prepared to trust Him yourself without a half-crown!" I was nearly choked. How gladly would I have compromised with my conscience if I had a florin (gold coin) and a sixpence! I would have given the florin thankfully and kept the rest, but I was not yet prepared to trust in God alone without the sixpence.

To talk was impossible under these circumstances. Yet, strange to say, I thought I should have no difficulty in praying. Prayer was a delightful occupation to me in those days. Time thus spent never seemed wearisome, and I knew nothing of lack of words. I seemed to think that all I should have to do would be to kneel down and engage in prayer, and relief would come to them and me together. "You asked me to come and pray with your wife," I said to the man, "so let us pray." And I knelt down. But scarcely had I opened my lips with "Our Father who art in heaven" than my conscience said, "Dare you mock God? Dare you kneel down and call Him Father with that half-crown in your pocket?" Such a time of conflict came upon me then as I have never experienced before nor since. How I got through that form of prayer I know not, and whether the words uttered were connected or disconnected, I cannot tell, but I arose from my knees in great distress of mind.

The poor father turned to me and said, "You see what a terrible state we are in, sir; if you can help us, for God's sake do!"

Just then the word flashed into my mind, *Give to him that asketh thee*, and in the word of a King, there is power. I put my hand into my pocket and, slowly drawing forth the half-crown, gave it to the man. I told him that it might seem a small matter for me to relieve them, seeing that I was comparatively well off, but that in parting with that coin, I was giving him my all. What I had been trying to tell him was indeed true – God really was a Father and might be trusted. The joy all came back in full flood tide to my heart; I could say anything and feel it then, and the hindrance to blessing was gone – gone, I trust, forever.

Not only was the poor woman's life saved, but I realized that my life was saved too. It might have been a wreck – would have been a wreck probably, as a Christian life – had not grace at that time conquered, and the striving of God's Spirit been obeyed. I well remember how that night, as I went home to my lodgings, my heart was as light as my pocket. The lonely, deserted streets resounded with a hymn of praise, which I could not restrain. When I took my basin of gruel before retiring, I would not have exchanged it for a prince's feast. I reminded the Lord as I knelt at my bedside of His own Word: He who giveth to the poor lendeth to the Lord. I asked Him not to let my loan be a long one, or I should have no dinner the next day; and with peace within and peace without, I spent a happy, restful night.

Next morning for breakfast, my plate of porridge remained, and before it was consumed, I heard the postman's knock at the door. I was not in the habit of receiving letters on Monday, as my parents and most of my friends refrained from posting on Saturday. So I was somewhat surprised when the landlady came in holding a letter or packet in her wet hand covered by her apron. I looked at the letter, but could not make out the handwriting. It was either a strange hand or a feigned one, and the postmark was blurred. Where it came from, I could not tell. On opening the envelope, I found nothing written within, but a pair of kid gloves was folded inside a sheet of blank paper, from which, as I opened them in astonishment, a half-sovereign (gold coin) fell to the ground. "Praise the Lord!" I exclaimed.

"Four hundred percent for twelve hours' investment; that is good interest. How glad the merchants of Hull would be if they could lend their money at such a rate!" I then and there determined that a bank which could not break should have my savings or earnings as the case might be – a determination I have not yet learned to regret.

I cannot tell you how often my mind has returned to this incident or all the help it has been to me in circumstances of difficulty in life afterward. If we are faithful to God in little things, we shall gain experience and strength that will be helpful to us in the more serious trials of life.

CHAPTER 4

Further Answers to Prayer

The remarkable and gracious deliverance I have spoken of was a great joy to me, as well as a strong confirmation of faith. But of course, ten shillings, however economically used, will not go very far, and it was nonetheless necessary to continue in prayer, asking that the larger supply which was still due might be remembered and paid. All my petitions, however, appeared to remain unanswered. Before a fortnight had elapsed, I found myself pretty much in the same position that I had occupied on that memorable Sunday night. Meanwhile, I continued pleading with God more and more earnestly that He would graciously remind my employer that my salary was overdue. Of course, it was not the want of the money that distressed me. That could have been had at any time for the asking. The question uppermost in my mind was this: "Can I go to China? Or will my want of faith and power with God prove to be so serious an obstacle as to preclude my entering upon this much-prized service?"

As the week drew to a close, I felt exceedingly agitated. There was not only myself to consider; on Saturday night, a payment would be due to my Christian landlady, which I knew she could not easily live without. Should I not, for her sake, speak about the matter of the salary? Yet, to do so would be, to myself at any rate, the admission that I was not fitted to undertake a missionary enterprise. I gave nearly the whole of Thursday and Friday (all the time not occupied in my necessary employment) to earnestly wrestling with God in prayer. But still on Saturday morning,

I was in the same position as before. And now my earnest cry was for guidance as to whether it was my duty to break silence and speak to my employer, or whether I should still continue to wait for the Father's time. As far as I could judge, I received the assurance that to wait for His time was best, and God in some way or other would intervene on my behalf. So I waited, my heart being now at rest and the burden gone.

About five o'clock that Saturday afternoon, when the doctor had finished writing his prescriptions and taken his last circuit for the day, he threw himself back in his armchair, as he was wont, and began to speak of the things of God. He was a truly Christian man, and we had many seasons of very happy spiritual fellowship together. I was busily watching a pan in which chowder was boiling that required a good deal of attention. It was indeed fortunate for me that it was, for without any obvious connection with what had been going on, all at once, he said, "By the bye, Taylor, is not your salary due again?"

My emotion may be imagined! I had to swallow two or three times before I could answer. With my eye fixed on the pan and my back to the doctor, I told him as quietly as I could that it was overdue some little time. How thankful I felt at that moment! God surely had heard my prayer and caused him, in this time of my great need, to remember the salary without any word or suggestion from me.

He replied, "Oh, I am so sorry you did not remind me! You know how busy I am; I wish I had thought of it a little sooner, for only this afternoon I sent all the money I had to the bank. Otherwise I would pay you at once." It is impossible to describe the despair caused by this unexpected statement. I knew not what to do. Fortunately for me, my pan boiled up, and I had a good reason for rushing with it from the room. Glad indeed I was to get away and keep out of sight until after the doctor had returned to his house. I was most thankful that he had not perceived my emotion.

As soon as he was gone, I had to seek my little sanctum and pour out my heart before the Lord for some time, before calmness, and more than calmness – thankfulness and joy, were restored to me. I felt that God had His own way and was not going to fail me. I had sought to know His will early in the day, and as far as I could judge, I had received guidance to wait patiently. Now God was going to work for me in some other way.

That evening was spent as my Saturday evenings usually were, in reading the Word and preparing the subjects on which I expected to speak in the various lodging houses the next day. I waited, perhaps a little longer than usual. At last, about ten o'clock, with no interruption of any kind, I put on my overcoat and prepared to leave for home, rather thankful to know that by the time I would let myself in with the latch key, my land-lady would have retired early to rest. There was certainly no help for that night, but perhaps God would intervene for me by Monday. I might be able to pay my landlady early in the week the money I would have given her before, if it had been possible.

Just as I was preparing to turn down the gas, I heard the doctor's step in the garden, which lay between the dwelling house and surgery. He was laughing to himself very heartily, as though greatly amused by something. Entering the surgery, he asked for the ledger and told me that, strange to say, one of his richest patients had just come to pay his doctor's bill. Was that not an odd thing to do? It never struck me that it might have any bearing on my own particular case, or I might have felt embarrassed. Looking at it simply from the position of an uninterested spectator, I also was highly amused that a man who was rolling in wealth should come after ten o'clock at night to pay a doctor's bill, which he could have paid by a check with the greatest ease any day. It appeared that somehow or other he could not rest with this on his mind; he had been constrained to come at that unusual hour to discharge his liability.

The account was receipted in the ledger, and the doctor was about to leave, when suddenly he turned and handed me some of the bank notes just received. To my surprise and thankfulness, he said, "By the way, Taylor, you might as well take these notes; I have not any change, but can give you the balance next week." Again, I was left with my feelings undiscovered to go back to my own little closet and praise the Lord with a joyful heart that after all I might go to China.

To me this incident was not a trivial one; to recall it sometimes in circumstances of great difficulty, in China or elsewhere, has proved no small comfort and strength.

By and by, the time drew near when it was thought desirable that I should leave Hull to attend the medical course of the London Hospital. A little while spent there and then I had every reason to believe that my life work in China would commence. But as much as I had rejoiced at the willingness of God to hear and answer prayer and to help His half-trusting, half-timid child, I felt that I could not go to China without having further developed and tested my power to rest upon His faithfulness. A marked opportunity for doing so was providentially granted to me.

My dear father had offered to bear all the expense of my stay in London. I knew, however, that due to recent losses, it would mean a considerable sacrifice for him to undertake this just when it seemed necessary for me to go forward. I had recently become acquainted with the Committee of the Chinese Evangelization Society with whom I ultimately left for China. I also met their secretary, my esteemed and much-loved friend Mr. George Pearse, then of the stock exchange, but now and for many years himself a missionary. Not knowing of my father's proposition, the Committee also kindly offered to bear my expenses while in London. When these proposals were first made to me, I was not quite clear as to what I ought to do. In writing to my father and the secretaries, I told them that I would take a few days to pray about the matter before deciding any course of action. I mentioned to my father that I'd received this offer from the Society, and I also told the secretaries of his offer of aid.

Subsequently, while waiting upon God in prayer for guidance, it became clear to my mind that I could decline both offers without difficulty. The secretaries of the Society would not know that I had cast myself wholly on God for supplies, and my father would conclude that I had accepted the other offer. I therefore wrote declining both propositions and felt that without anyone having either care or anxiety on my account, I was simply in the hands of God, and if He, who knew my heart, wished to encourage me to go to China, He would bless my effort to depend upon Him alone at home.

CHAPTER 5

Life in London

Imust not now attempt to detail the ways in which the Lord was pleased – often to my surprise, as well as to my delight – to help me from time to time. I soon found that it was not possible to live quite as economically in London as in Hull. To lessen expenses, I shared a room with a cousin, four miles from the hospital, providing myself with board. After various experiments, I found that the most economical way was to live almost exclusively on brown bread and water. Thus, I was able to make the means that God gave me last as long as possible. Some of my expenses I could not diminish, but my board was largely within my own control. A large two-penny loaf of brown bread, purchased daily on my long walk from the hospital, furnished me with supper and breakfast. On that diet, with a few apples for lunch, I managed to walk eight or nine miles a day and stand a good deal of time while attending the practice in the hospital and the medical school.

One incident that occurred about this time I must mention. The husband of my former landlady in Hull was chief officer of a ship that sailed from London, and by receiving his half-pay monthly and remitting it to her, I was able to save her the cost of a commission. I had been doing this for several months, when she wrote requesting that I should obtain the next payment as early as possible, as her rent was almost due, and she depended upon that sum to meet it. The request came at an inconvenient time. I was working hard for an examination in the hope of obtaining a scholarship, which would be of service to me, and felt that I could not afford the time to go during the busiest part of the day to the city and procure the money. I had, however, sufficient of my own money in hand to enable me to send the required sum. I made the remittance, therefore, intending to go and draw the regular allowance as soon as the examination was over and refund myself.

Before the time of examination, the medical school was closed for a day for the funeral of the Duke of Wellington, and I had an opportunity to go at once to the office, which was situated on a street in Cheapside, and apply for the due amount. To my surprise and dismay, the cleric told me that he could not pay it, as the officer in question had run away from his ship and gone to the gold diggings.

"Well," I remarked, "that is very inconvenient for me, as I have already advanced the money, and I know his wife will have no means of repaying it."

The clerk said he was sorry, but could of course only act according to orders. So there was no help for me in that direction. A little more time and thought, however, brought a comforting conclusion to my mind. I was depending on the Lord for everything, and His means were not limited. It was a small matter to be brought a little sooner or later into the position of needing fresh supplies from Him, so the joy and the peace were not long interfered with.

Very soon after this, possibly the same evening, while sewing together some sheets of paper on which to take notes of the lectures, I accidentally pricked the first finger of my right hand. In a few moments, I forgot all about it. The next day at the hospital, I continued dissecting as before. The body was that of a person who had died of fever and was more than usually disagreeable and dangerous. I need scarcely say that those of us who were working on it dissected with special care, knowing that the slightest scratch might cost us our lives. Before the morning was far advanced, I began to feel very weary. While going through the surgical wards at noon, I was obliged to run out, being suddenly very sick, a most unusual circumstance with me. I only took a little food and nothing that could disagree with me. After feeling faint for some time, a draught of cold water revived me, and I was able to rejoin the students. I became more and more ill, however, and when the afternoon lecture on surgery was over, I found it impossible to hold the pencil and continue taking notes. By the time the next lecture was through, my whole arm and right side were full of severe pain, and I was looking and feeling very ill.

Finding that I could not resume work, I went into the dissecting room to bind up the portion I was involved with and put away my apparatus. I said to the demonstrator, who was a very skillful surgeon, "I cannot think what has come over me," as I described the symptoms.

"Why," said he, "what has happened is clear enough: you must have cut yourself in dissecting, and you know that this is a case of malignant fever." I assured him that I had been most careful and was quite certain that I had no cut or scratch. "Well," he replied, "you certainly must have had one." He very closely scrutinized my hand to find it, but in vain.

All at once, it occurred to me that I had pricked my finger the night before, and I asked him if it were possible that a prick from a needle at that time could have been open. His opinion was that this was probably the cause of the trouble, and he advised me to get a hansom (horse-drawn vehicle), drive home as fast as I could, and arrange my affairs forthwith. "For," he said, "you are a dead man."

My first thought was one of sorrow that I could not go to China, but very soon came the feeling: "Unless I am greatly mistaken, I have work to do in China and shall not die." I was glad, however, to take the opportunity of speaking to my medical friend. He was a confirmed skeptic of things spiritual and the joy that the prospect of perhaps soon being with my Master gave me. At the same time I told him that I did not think I should die, for unless I was mistaken, I had work to do in China, and however severe the struggle, I must be brought through.

"That is all very well," he answered, "but you get a hansom and drive home as fast as you can. You have no time to lose, for you will soon be incapable of winding up your affairs."

I smiled a little at the idea of my driving home in a hansom, for by this time my means were too exhausted to allow such a proceeding, and I set out to walk the distance if possible. Before long, however, my strength gave way, and I felt it was no use to attempt to reach home by walking. I availed myself of an omnibus from Whitechapel Church to Farringdon Street and another from Farringdon Street onwards. With great suffering, I reached the neighborhood of Soho Square, behind which I lived. Upon entering the house, I got some hot water from the servant and charged her very earnestly – literally as a dying man – to accept eternal life as the gift of God through Jesus Christ. I bathed my head and lanced the finger, hoping to let out some of the poisoned blood. The pain was very severe; I fainted and was unconscious for some time – so long that when I came to, I found that I had been carried to bed.

An uncle of mine who lived near had come in and sent for his own medical man, an assistant surgeon at the Westminster Hospital. I assured my uncle that medical help would be of no service to me, and I did not wish to go to the expense involved. He, however, quieted me on this account, saying that he had sent for his own doctor, and the bill would be charged to him.

When the surgeon came and learned all the particulars, he said, "Well, if you have been living moderately, you may pull through; but if you have been going in for beer and that sort of thing, there is no manner of chance for you."

I thought that if sober living was to do anything, few could have a better chance, as little but bread and water had been my diet for a good while. I told him I had lived sparingly and found that it helped me in study.

"But now," he said, "you must keep up your strength, for it will be a pretty hard struggle." And he ordered me a bottle of port wine every day and as many chops as I could consume. Again, I smiled inwardly, having no means for the purchase of such luxuries. This difficulty, however, was also met by my kind uncle, who sent me at once all that was needed.

I was concerned, in addition to the agony I suffered, that my dear parents should not be made aware of my state. Thought and prayer had satisfied me that I was not going to die, for there was indeed a work for me to do in China. If my dear parents should come up and find me in that condition, I would lose the opportunity of seeing how God was going to work for me now that my money had almost come to an end. So, after prayer for guidance, I obtained a promise from my uncle and cousin not to write to my parents, but to allow me to communicate with them myself. I felt it was a very distinct answer to prayer when they gave me this promise, and I took care to handle all communication with them until the crisis was past and the worst of the attack was over. At home, they knew that I was working hard for an examination and did not wonder at my silence.

Days and nights of suffering passed slowly, but at length, after several weeks, I was sufficiently restored to leave my room. Then I learned that two men, though not from the London Hospital, who'd had dissection wounds at the same time as myself, had both succumbed, while I was spared in answer to prayer for the work for God in China.

Water gate and Custom house, Soo-chow

CHAPTER 6

Strengthened by Faith

One day the doctor came and found me on the sofa; he was surprised to learn that with assistance I had walked downstairs. "Now," he said, "the best thing you can do is to go to the countryside as soon as you feel up to the journey. You must withdraw until you have recovered a fair amount of health and strength, for if you begin your work too soon, the consequences may still be serious."

When he had left, as I lay very exhausted on the sofa, I just told the Lord all about it. I would refrain from making my circumstances known to those who would delight to meet my need, in order that my faith might be strengthened by receiving help from Him in answer to prayer alone. What was I to do? And I waited for His answer.

It seemed to me as if He were directing my mind to the conclusion to go again to the shipping office and inquire about the wages I had been unable to draw. I reminded the Lord that I could not afford to take a carriage, and it did not seem at all likely that I would succeed in getting the money. I asked whether this impulse was not a mere clutching at a straw, some mental process of my own, rather than His guidance and teaching. After prayer, however, and renewed waiting upon God, I was confirmed in my belief that He was telling me to go to the office.

The next question was, "How am I to go?" I had to seek help in going downstairs, and the place was at least two miles away. The assurance was brought vividly home to me that whatever I asked of God in the name of Christ would be done, that the

Father might be glorified in the Son. What I had to do was to seek strength for the long walk, receive it by faith, and set out upon it. Unhesitatingly, I told the Lord that I was quite willing to take the walk if He would give me the strength. I asked in the name of Christ that the strength might be immediately given, and sending the servant up to my room for my hat and stick, I set out, not to *attempt* to walk, but to walk to Cheapside.

Although undoubtedly strengthened by faith, I never took so much interest in shop windows as I did upon that journey. At every second or third step, I was glad to lean a little against the plate glass and take time to examine the contents in the windows before passing on. It needed a special effort of faith when I got to the bottom of Farringdon Street to attempt the toilsome ascent of Snow Hill. There was no Holborn Viaduct in those days, and the ascent had to be made. God did help me, and in due time I reached Cheapside, turned into the side street in which the office was found, and sat down very exhausted on the steps leading to the first floor, which was my destination. I felt my position to be a little peculiar – sitting there on the steps, so evidently spent – and the gentlemen who rushed up and down stairs looked at me with an inquiring gaze. After a little rest, however, and a further season of prayer, I succeeded in climbing the staircase. To my comfort, I found the clerk with whom I had hitherto dealt in the matter. Seeing me looking pale and exhausted, he kindly inquired as to my health, and I told him that I had a serious illness and was ordered to the countryside, but thought it well to call first and make further inquiry, lest there should have been any mistake about the mate having run off to the gold diggings.

"Oh," he said, "I am so glad you have come, for it turns out that it was an able seaman of the same name that ran away. The mate is still on board; the ship has just reached Gravesend and will be up very soon. I shall be glad to give you the half-pay up to date, for doubtless it will reach his wife more safely through you. We all know what temptations beset the men when they arrive at home after a voyage."

Before giving me the sum of money, however, he insisted upon my coming inside and sharing his lunch. I felt it was the Lord indeed who was providing for me and accepted his offer with thankfulness. When I was refreshed and rested, he gave me a sheet of paper to write a few lines to the wife, telling her of the circumstances. On my way back, I procured a money order in Cheapside for the balance due to her and posted it. Returning home again, I felt myself quite justified in taking an omnibus as far as it would serve me.

Feeling much better the next morning, after seeing to some little matters that I had to settle, I made my way to the surgery of the doctor who had attended me. I felt that, although my uncle was prepared to pay the bill, it was right for me, now that I had some money in hand, to ask for the account myself. The kind surgeon refused to allow me, as a medical student, to pay anything for his attendance. He did allow me to pay for the quinine he supplied to the extent of eight shillings. When that was settled, I saw that the sum left was just sufficient to take me home, and to my mind the whole thing seemed a wonderful intervention of God on my behalf.

I knew that the surgeon was skeptical, but I told him I should like to speak to him freely, if I might do so without offense. I felt that under God I owed my life to his kind care and wished very earnestly that he himself might become a partaker of the same precious faith that I possessed. So I told him my purpose for being in London, my circumstances, and the reason I had declined the help of both my father and the officers of the Society in connection with my possible mission to China. I told him of the recent providential dealings of God with me and how apparently hopeless my position had been the day before, when he had ordered me to go to the countryside. I described to him the mental exercises I had gone through, but when I added that I actually got up from the sofa and walked to Cheapside, he looked at me incredulously and said, "Impossible! Why, I left you lying there more like a ghost than a man." I had to assure him again and again that, strengthened by faith, I had really taken the walk. I also told him what money was left to me and what payments had to be made, and I showed him that just sufficient moneys remained to take me home to Yorkshire, providing for needful refreshment by the way and the omnibus journey at the end.

My kind friend was completely broken down and said with tears in his eyes, "I would give all the world for a faith like yours."

I, on the other hand, had the joy of telling him that it was to be obtained without money and without price. We never met again. When I came back to town, restored to health and strength, I found that he'd had a stroke and left for the countryside. I subsequently learned that he never rallied. I was able to gain no information as to his state of mind when taken away, but I have always felt very thankful that I had the opportunity, and embraced it, of bearing that testimony for God. I cannot but entertain the hope that the Master Himself was speaking to him through His dealings with me, and that I shall meet him again in the Better Land. It would be no small joy to be welcomed by him, when my own service is over.

The next day found me in my dear parents' home. My joy in the Lord's help and deliverance was so great that I was unable to keep it to myself, and before my return to London, my dear mother knew the secret of my past life. I need scarcely say that when I went up again to town, I was not allowed to live – indeed, I was not fit to live – on the same economical means as before my illness. I needed more now, and the Lord did provide.

Temple and memorial portal

CHAPTER 7

Mighty to Save

Returning to London when sufficiently recovered, I resumed the busy life of hospital and lecture hall. Happy Sundays of fellowship with Christian friends, especially in London or Tottenham, often brought relief. Opportunities for service are to be found in every sphere, and mine was no exception. I shall only mention one case now that gave me great encouragement in seeking conversion even when it seemed apparently hopeless.

God had given me the joy of winning souls before, but not in surroundings of such special difficulty. With God all things are possible, and no conversion ever takes place save by the almighty power of the Holy Ghost. The great need, therefore, of every Christian worker is to *know* God. Indeed, this is the purpose for which He has given us eternal life, as our Savior Himself says in the often-misquoted verse, John 17:3: *And this is* [the object of] *life eternal,* [not to know but] *that they might know thee the only true God, and Jesus Christ, whom thou hast sent.* I was now to prove the willingness of God to answer prayer for spiritual blessing under most unpromising circumstances and thus gain an increased acquaintance with the prayer-answering God as One *mighty to save.*

A short time before leaving for China, it became my daily duty to dress the foot of a patient suffering from senile gangrene. The disease commenced, as usual, insidiously, and the patient had little idea that he was a doomed man with not long to live. I was not the first to attend to him, but when the case was transferred to me, I naturally became very anxious about his soul. The family with whom he lived were Christians, and from them I learned that he was an avowed atheist and very antagonistic to anything religious. Without asking his consent, they had invited a Scripture reader to visit him, but in great passion he had ordered him from the room. The vicar of the district had also called, hoping to help him, but he had spit in his face and refused to allow him to speak. His passionate temper was described to me as very violent, and altogether the case seemed to be as hopeless as could be imagined.

When I first attended to him, I prayed much about it, but for two or three days said nothing to him of a religious nature. By special care in dressing his diseased limb, I was able to lessen his suffering considerably, and he soon showed grateful appreciation of my services. One day, with a trembling heart, I took advantage of his warm acknowledgments to tell him what caused my actions and speak of his own solemn position and need of God's mercy through Christ. It was only by a powerful effort of self-restraint that he kept his lips closed. He turned over in bed with his back to me and uttered no word.

I could not get the poor man out of my mind, and very often through each day, I pleaded with God, by His Spirit, to save him before He took him. After dressing the wound and relieving his pain, I never failed to say a few words to him, which I hoped the Lord would bless. He always turned his back to me, looking annoyed, but never spoke a word in reply.

After continuing this for some time, my heart sank. It seemed to me that I was not only doing no good but, perhaps, hardening him and increasing his guilt. One day, after dressing his limb and washing my hands, instead of returning to the bedside to speak to him, I went to the door and stood hesitating for a few moments with the thought in my mind: "Ephraim is joined to his idols; let him alone." I looked at the man and saw his surprise, as it was the first time since speaking to him that I had attempted to leave without going up to his bedside to say a few words for my Master. I could bear it no longer. Bursting into tears, I crossed the room and said, "My friend, whether you will hear or whether you will forbear, I *must* deliver *my* soul," and went on to speak very earnestly to him, telling him with many tears how much I wished that he would let me pray with him.

To my unspeakable joy, he did not turn away but replied, "If it will be a relief to you, do." I need scarcely say that I fell on my knees and poured out my whole soul to God on his behalf. I believe the Lord wrought a change in his soul then and there.

After this, he was never unwilling to be spoken to and prayed with, and within a few days he definitely accepted Christ as his Savior. Oh, the joy it was to me to see that dear man rejoicing in hope of the glory of God! He told me that for forty years he had never darkened the door of a church or chapel, and then, forty years ago, he had only entered a place of worship to be married. He could not even be persuaded to go inside when his wife was buried. Now, thank God, I had every reason to believe his sin-stained soul was washed, was sanctified, and was justified in the name of the Lord Jesus Christ and in the Spirit of our God. Oftentimes, when in my early work in China, circumstances rendered me almost hopeless of success, I have thought of this man's conversion and have been encouraged to persevere in speaking the Word, whether men would hear or whether they would forbear.

The now-happy sufferer lived for some time after this change and was never tired of bearing testimony to the grace of God. Though his condition was most distressing, the alteration in his character and behavior made the previously painful duty of attending him one of real pleasure. I have often thought since, in connection with this case and the work of God generally, of the words: *He that goeth forth and weepeth, bearing precious seed, shall doubtless come again with rejoicing, bringing his sheaves with him.* Perhaps if there were more of that intense distress for souls that leads to tears, we would see the results we desire more frequently. Sometimes it may be that while we are complaining of the hardness of the hearts of those we are seeking to benefit, the hardness of our own hearts and our own feeble apprehension of the solemn reality of eternal things may be the true cause of our lack of success.

CHAPTER 8

Voyage to China

Soon after this, the time I so long looked forward to, arrived – the time to leave England for China. After being set apart with many prayers for the ministry of God's Word among the heathen Chinese, I left London for Liverpool. On the nineteenth of September 1853, a little service was held in the stern cabin of the *Dumfries*, which had been secured for me by the Committee of the Chinese Evangelization Society, under whose administration I was going to China.

My beloved mother had come to see me off from Liverpool. Never shall I forget that day or how she went with me into the little cabin that was to be my home for nearly six long months. With a mother's loving hand, she smoothed the little bed. She sat by my side and joined me in the last hymn that we should sing together before the parting. We knelt down, and she prayed – my mother's last prayer I was to hear before starting for China. Then notice was given that we must separate, and we had to say good-bye, never expecting to meet on earth again.

For my sake, she restrained her feelings as much as possible. We parted, and she went on shore, giving me her blessing. I stood alone on deck, and she followed the ship as we moved towards the dock gates. As we passed through the gates and the separation commenced, the cry of anguish that wrung from her heart shall stay with me forever. It went through me like a knife. I never knew so fully, until then, what *God so loved the world* meant. And I am quite sure that my precious mother learned more of the love of God for the perishing in that hour than in all her life before.

Oh, how it must grieve the heart of God when He sees His children indifferent to the needs of that wide world for which His beloved, His only begotten Son, died!

> *Hearken, O daughter, and consider, and incline thine ear; forget also thine own people, and thy father's house; So shall the king greatly desire thy beauty: for he is thy Lord; and worship thou him.*
> (Psalm 45:10-11)

Praise God, the number is increasing who are discovering the exceeding joys and the wondrous revelations of His mercies, bestowed on those who follow Him. They are emptying themselves and leaving all in obedience to His Great Commission.

It was on September 19, 1853, that the *Dumfries* sailed for China. I did not arrive in Shanghai until March 1, 1854, the spring of the following year.

Our voyage had a rough beginning, but many had promised to remember us in constant prayer. This was no small comfort, for we had scarcely left the Mersey when a violent equinoctial gale caught us. For twelve days, we were beating backwards and forwards in the Irish Channel, unable to get out to sea. The gale steadily increased, and after almost a week, we lay to for a time. But drifting on a lee coast, we were compelled again to make sail and endeavored to beat on to windward. The utmost efforts of the captain and crew, however, were to no avail, and Sunday night, September 25, 1853, found us drifting into Caernarvon Bay, each tack becoming shorter, until at last we were within a stone's throw of the rocks. About this time, the ship, which had refused to stay, was put around in the other direction. The Christian captain said to me, "We cannot live half an hour now. What of your call to labor for the Lord in China?"

I had previously passed through a time of much conflict, but that was over. It was a great joy to tell him that I would not want to be in any other position. I strongly expected to reach China, but if otherwise, the Master would say it was well that I was found seeking to obey His command.

Within a few minutes after wearing ship, the captain walked up to the compass and said to me, "The wind has freed two points; we shall be able to beat out of the bay." And so we did. The bowsprit was sprung, and the vessel seriously strained, but in a few days we got out to sea, and the necessary repairs were thoroughly effected on board without causing any further delay.

One thing was a great trouble to me that night. I was a very young believer and did not have sufficient faith in God to see Him in and through any means. I had felt it my duty to comply with the earnest wish of my beloved and honored mother and procure a swimming belt. But in my own soul, I felt as if I could not simply trust in God while I had this swimming belt. My heart had no rest until on that night, after all hope of being saved was gone, I had given it away. Then I had perfect peace; and, strange to say, I put several light things together to float at the time we struck, without any thought of inconsistency or scruple. Ever since, I have seen clearly the mistake I made, a mistake that is very common in these days, when erroneous teaching on faith healing does much harm, misleading some as to the purposes of God, shaking the faith of others, and distressing the minds of many. The use of means should not lessen our faith in God; and our faith in God should not hinder us from using whatever means He has given us for the accomplishment of His own purposes.

For years after this, I always took a swimming belt with me and never had any trouble about it. After the storm was over, the question was settled for me through the prayerful study of the Scriptures. God allowed me to see my mistake, probably to deliver me from a great deal of trouble on similar questions now so constantly raised. When in medical or surgical charge of any case, I have never thought of neglecting to ask God's guidance and blessing in the use of appropriate means or failing to give Him thanks for answered prayer and restored health. But to me, it would appear as presumptuous and wrong to neglect the use of those measures, which He Himself has put within our reach as to neglect to take daily food and suppose that life and health might be maintained by prayer alone.

The voyage was a tedious one. We lost a good deal of time on the equator from calms, and when we finally reached the Eastern Archipelago, we were again detained for the same reason. Usually a breeze would spring up soon after sunset and last until about dawn. The utmost use was made of it, but during the day we lay still with flapping sails, often drifting back and losing a good deal of the advantage we had gained during the night.

This happened notably on one occasion, when we were in dangerous proximity to the north of New Guinea. Saturday night had brought us to a point some thirty miles off the land, but during the Sunday morning service, which was held on deck, I could not fail to notice that the captain looked troubled and frequently went over to the side of the ship. When the service was ended, I learned that a four-knot current was carrying us rapidly towards some sunken reefs. We were already so near that it seemed improbable we should get through the afternoon safely. After dinner, the long boat was put out, and all hands endeavored, without success, to turn the ship's head from the shore. As we drifted nearer, we could plainly see the natives rushing about the sands and lighting fires here and there. The captain's hornbook informed him that these people were cannibals, so our position was quite alarming.

After standing together on the deck for some time in silence, the captain said to me, "Well, we have done everything that can be done; we can only await the result."

A thought occurred to me, and I replied, "No, there is one thing we have not done yet."

"What is it?" he queried.

"Four of us on board are Christians," I answered (the Swedish carpenter and our colored steward with the captain and myself). "Let us each retire to our own cabin and in prayer ask the Lord to give us immediately a breeze. He can send it now as easily as at sunset."

The captain complied with this proposal. I went and spoke to the other two men, and after prayer with the carpenter, we all four retired to wait upon God. I had a good but very brief season in prayer and then felt so satisfied that our request was granted that I could not continue asking. Very soon I went up again on deck. The first officer, a godless man, was in charge. I went over and asked him to let down the clews or corners of the mainsail, which had been drawn up in order to lessen the useless flapping of the sail against the rigging.

He answered, "What would be the good of that?"

I told him we had been asking for a wind from God, and it was coming immediately. We were so near the reef by this time that there was not a minute to lose. With a look of incredulity and contempt and an oath, he said that he would rather see a wind than hear of it! But while he was speaking, I watched his eye and followed it up to the royal (the topmost sail), and there, sure enough, the corner of the sail was beginning to tremble in the coming breeze.

"Don't you see the wind is coming? Look at the royal!" I exclaimed.

"No, it is only a cat's-paw," he rejoined (a mere puff of wind).

"Cat's-paw or not," I cried, "I pray you, let down the mainsail, and let us have the benefit!"

He was not slow to do this. In another minute, the heavy tread of the men on the deck brought the captain up from his cabin to see what was the matter. He saw that the breeze had indeed come. In a few minutes, we were ploughing our way at six or seven knots an hour through the water, and the multitude of naked savages we had seen on the beach had no wreckage that night. We were soon out of danger, and though the wind was sometimes unsteady, we did not lose it altogether until after passing the Pelew Islands.

Thus God encouraged me, before landing on China's shores, to bring every variety of need to Him in prayer and *to expect that He would honor the name* of the Lord Jesus and give the help which each emergency required.

CHAPTER 9

Early Missionary Experiences

On landing in Shanghai on March 1, 1854, I was surrounded with difficulties that were wholly unexpected. A band of rebels, known as the "Red Turbans," had taken possession of the native city, against which an Imperial army of forty to fifty thousand men was encamped. They were a much greater source of discomfort and danger to the little European community than were the rebels themselves. Upon landing, I was told that living outside the Settlement was impossible, but within, the foreign concession apartments were scarcely obtainable at any price. The dollar, now worth about three shillings, had risen to a value of eight and nine pence. The prospect for an apartment with only a small income of English money was dark indeed. However, I had three letters of introduction and depended on counsel and help, especially from one of those to whom I had been commended, whose friends I knew well and highly valued. Of course, I sought him out at once, only to learn that he had been buried a month or two before, having died from fever during the time of my voyage.

Saddened by these tidings, I inquired for a missionary to whom another of my letters of introduction was addressed, but a further disappointment awaited me. He had left for America. The third letter remained, but as it had been given by a comparative stranger, I had expected less from it than from the other two. It proved, however, to be God's channel of help. The Rev. Dr. Medhurst of the London Mission, to whom it was addressed, introduced me to Dr. Lockhart. He kindly allowed me to live with him for six months. Dr. Medhurst procured my first Chinese teacher, and he, Dr. Edkins, and the late Mr. Alexander Wylie gave me considerable help with the language.

Those were indeed troublesome times and times of danger. Coming out of the city one day with Mr. Wylie, he entered into conversation with two coolies, while we waited at the East Gate for a companion who was behind us. Before our companion came, an attack upon the city from the batteries on the opposite side of the river commenced, which caused us to hurry away to a place of less danger. The whiz of the balls was unpleasantly near. The coolies, unfortunately, stayed too long and were wounded. On reaching the Settlement, we stopped for a few minutes to make a purchase and then proceeded at once to the London Mission compound. At the door of the hospital, we found the two poor coolies with whom Mr. Wylie had conversed, their four ankles terribly shattered by a cannon ball. The poor fellows declined amputation and both died. We recognized how narrow our escape had been.

At another time, early in the morning, I had joined one of the missionaries on his veranda to watch the battle proceeding at a distance of perhaps three-quarters of a mile. Suddenly, a spent ball passed between us and buried itself in the veranda wall. On another day, my friend Mr. Wylie left a book on the table after lunch, and returning for it about five minutes later, he found the arm of the chair on which he had been sitting shot clean away. But in the midst of these and many other dangers, God protected us.

After six months' stay with Dr. Lockhart, I rented a native house outside the Settlement and commenced a little missionary work amongst my Chinese neighbors, which continued workable for a few months. When the French joined the Imperialists in attacking the city, the position of my house became so dangerous that during the last few weeks, because of nightly recurring skirmishes, I gave up attempting to sleep except in the daytime. One night a fire appeared very near, and I climbed up to a little observatory I had arranged on the roof of the house to see whether it was necessary to attempt escape. While there, a ball struck the ridge of the roof on the opposite side of the quadrangle, showering pieces of broken tile all around me. The ball itself rolled down into the court below. It weighed four or five pounds, and had it come a few inches higher, it would probably have spent its force on me instead of on the building. My dear mother kept the ball for many years. Shortly after this, I had to abandon the house and return to the Foreign Settlement – a step that was taken none too soon, for before the last of my belongings were removed, the house was burned to the ground.

It is scarcely possible to convey any adequate idea of the trials of this early period. To one of a sensitive nature, the horrors, atrocities, and misery connected with war were a terrible ordeal. The embarrassment of the times was also considerable. With an income of only eighty pounds a year, I was compelled to give one hundred and twenty for rent and sublet half the house when I moved into the Settlement. The Committee of the Chinese Evangelization Society learned of our circumstances after the arrival of Dr. Parker and increased my income. However, many painful experiences had already taken place. Few can realize how distressing these difficulties seemed to a young, untried worker. With the intense loneliness of the position of a pioneer, he could not even hint at many of his circumstances, as to do so would have been an unspoken appeal for help.

The great Enemy is always ready with his often-repeated suggestion: "All these things are against me." But oh, how false the word! The cold, the hunger, the watchings, the sleeplessness in nights of danger, and the utter isolation and helplessness were wisely chosen and tenderly and lovingly meted out. What circumstances could have rendered the Word of God sweeter, the presence of God more real, and the help of God more precious? These were times of emptying and humbling, but they were also experiences that made one not ashamed, and strengthened the purpose to go forward as God might direct with His *proven* promise: *I will not fail thee, nor forsake thee.* One can see, even now, that as for God, His way is perfect, and yet we can rejoice that the missionary path of today is comparatively a smooth and easy one.

Journeying inland was contrary to treaty arrangements and accompanied with much difficulty, especially for some time after the Battle of Muddy Flat. In this operation, an Anglo-American contingent of about three hundred marines and seamen with a volunteer corps of less than a hundred residents attacked the Imperial camp. They drove thirty to fifty thousand Chinese soldiers away, for the range of our shot and shell made the native artillery useless. Still, in the autumn of 1854, a journey of perhaps a week's duration was safely accomplished with Dr. Edkins, who of course did the speaking and preaching, while I was able to help in the distribution of books.

CHAPTER 10

First Evangelistic Efforts

A journey taken in the spring of 1855 with the Rev. J. S. Burden of the Church Missionary Society (now the Bishop of Victoria, Hong Kong) brought some serious dangers.

In the great mouth of the Yangtze River, some thirty miles to the north of Shanghai, lies the group of islands of which Tsung-ming and Hai-Men are the largest and most important. Farther up the river, where the estuary narrows away from the sea, is situated the influential city of Tung Chau, close to Lang Shan or the Wolf Mountains, famous as a resort for pilgrim devotees. We spent some time in evangelizing on those islands and then proceeded to Lang Shan, where we preached and gave books to thousands of the devotees who were attending an idolatrous festival. From thence, we went on to Tung Chau, and the following journal will tell of our painful experiences there:

Thursday, April 26, 1855

After breakfast, we committed ourselves to the care of our heavenly Father and sought His blessing before proceeding to this great city. The day was dull and wet. We felt persuaded that Satan would not allow us to assail his kingdom, as we were attempting to do, without raising serious opposition, but we were also fully assured that it was the will of God that we should preach Christ in this city and distribute the Word of Truth among its people. We were sorry that we only had a few books left for such an important place. The result, however, proved that this also was providential.

Our native teachers did their best to persuade us not to go into the city, but we determined that with God's help, nothing should hinder us. We directed them, however, to remain in one of the boats, and if we did not return, to learn whatever they could about our fate and hurry to Shanghai with the information. We also arranged for the other boat to wait for us, even if we could not get back that night, so we might not be detained for want of a boat if we were late. We then put our books into two bags, and with a servant who always accompanied us on these occasions, set off for the city, about seven miles away. Walking was out of the question due to the state of the roads, so we availed ourselves of wheelbarrows, the only vehicle to be had in these parts. A wheelbarrow is cheaper than a sedan, only requiring one coolie, but it is by no means an agreeable carriage on rough, dirty roads.

We had not gone far before a servant requested permission to go back, as he was thoroughly frightened by reports concerning the native soldiers. Of course, we consented, not wishing to involve another in trouble against his will.

At this point, a respectable man came up and earnestly warned us against proceeding. He said that if we continued, we would find to our sorrow what the Tung Chau militia was like. We thanked him for his kindly counsel but could not act upon it, as our hearts were fixed. It did not matter whether we were led to bonds, imprisonment, or death, or whether we could distribute our Scriptures and tracts in safety and return unhurt. We did not know, but we were determined, by the grace of God, not to leave Tung Chau any longer without the gospel or its teeming thousands to die in uncared-for ignorance of the Way of life.

After this, my wheelbarrow man would proceed no farther, and I had to seek another, who was fortunately not difficult to find. As we went on, the ride in the mud and rain was anything but agreeable, and we could not help feeling the danger of our position, but we never wavered for a moment. At intervals, we encouraged one another with promises from Scripture and verses of hymns. One verse seemed particularly appropriate to our circumstances, and was very comforting to me:

> The perils of the sea, the perils of the land,
> Should not dishearten thee: thy Lord is nigh at hand.
> But should thy courage fail, when tried and sore oppressed,
> His promise shall avail, and set thy soul at rest.

On our way, we passed through one small town of about a thousand inhabitants. In the Mandarin dialect, I preached Jesus to a good number of people here. Never was I so happy in speaking of the love of God and the atonement of Jesus Christ. My own soul was richly blessed and filled with joy and peace, and I was able to speak with unusual freedom and ease. And how I rejoiced when, afterwards, I heard one from our crowd repeating to the newcomers, in his own local dialect, the truths I had been sharing. Oh, how thankful I felt to hear a Chinaman, of his own accord, telling his fellow countrymen that God loved them, that they were sinners, but Jesus died in their place and paid the penalty of their guilt. That one moment repaid me for all the trials we had passed through, and I felt that if the Lord should grant His Holy Spirit to change the heart of that man, we had not come in vain.

We distributed a few Testaments and tracts, for the people were able to read, because we could not leave them without the gospel. It was to our advantage that we did so, for when we reached Tung Chau, we had as many left as we had strength to carry.

Nearing the end of our journey, as we approached the western suburb of the city, the prayer of the early Christians, when persecution was commencing, came to my mind: "And now, Lord, behold their threatenings and grant unto Thy servants that with all boldness they may speak Thy Word." In this petition, we most heartily united. Before entering the suburb, we laid our plans, so we could act in concert. We told our wheelbarrow men where to wait for us, so they might not be involved in any trouble on our account. Then, looking up to our heavenly Father, we committed ourselves to His keeping, took our books, and set on for the city.

For some distance, we walked along the principal street of the suburb leading to the West Gate unmolested and amused at the unusual title of *Heh-kwei-tsi* ("black devils") which was being applied to us. We wondered about it at the time, but afterwards found that it was our clothes and not our skin that gave rise to it. As we passed several of the soldiers, I remarked to Mr. Burdon that these were the men we had heard so much about and they seemed willing to receive us quietly enough. Long before we reached the gate, however, a tall, powerful man, made tenfold fiercer by partial intoxication, seized Mr. Burdon by the shoulders and let us know that all the militia were not so peaceably inclined. My companion endeavored to shake him off. I turned to see what the problem was, and at once we were surrounded by a dozen or more brutal men, who hurried us on to the city at a fearful pace.

My bag began to feel very heavy, and I could not change hands to relieve myself. I was soon perspiring profusely and scarcely able to keep up with them. We demanded to be taken before the chief magistrate, but we were told they knew where to take us. With the most insulting obscenity, they said they knew what to do with persons such as us. The man who first seized Mr. Burdon soon left him for me and became my principal tormentor. I was neither as tall nor as strong as my friend and was therefore less able to resist him. He all but knocked me down again and again, seized me by the hair, took hold of my collar so as to almost choke me, and grasped my arms and shoulders, making them black and blue. Had this treatment continued much longer, I would have fainted. Almost exhausted, the remembrance of a verse quoted by my dear mother in one of my last home letters refreshed me:

> We speak of the realms of the blest,
> That country so bright and so fair,
> And oft are its glories confessed;
> But what must it be to be there!

To be absent from the body! To be present with the Lord! To be free from sin! This would be the worst result that man's malice could ever bring upon us.

As we were walking along, Mr. Burdon tried to give away a few books that he was carrying, not knowing whether we might have another opportunity of doing so. The fearful rage of the soldier and the way he insisted on shackles being brought, which fortunately were not available, convinced us that in our present position we could do no good by attempting book distribution. There was nothing to be done but quietly to submit and go along with our captors.

Once or twice a quarrel arose over how to deal with us. The milder of our abductors said we ought to be taken to the magistrate's office, but others wished to kill us at once without appeal to any authority. Our minds were kept in perfect peace. When thrown together on one of these occasions, we reminded each other that the apostles rejoiced that they were counted *worthy* to suffer for the cause of Christ. Having succeeded in getting my hand into my pocket, I produced a Chinese card (if that is what you call the large red paper bearing one's name), and after this I was treated with more respect. I demanded it should be given to the chief official of the place, and that we should be led to his office. Before this, we had been unable, say what we would, to persuade them that we were foreigners, although we were both in English attire.

Oh, the long, weary streets that we were dragged through! I thought they would never end. Seldom have I felt more thankful than when we stopped at a place where we were told a mandarin resided. Quite exhausted, bathed in perspiration, and with my tongue cleaving to the roof of my mouth, I leaned against the wall and saw that Mr. Burdon was in much the same condition. I requested them to bring us chairs, but they told us to wait. When I begged them to give us some tea, I received the same answer. A large crowd had gathered around the doorway, and Mr. Burdon, collecting his remaining strength, preached Jesus Christ to them. Our cards and books had been taken to the mandarin, but he proved to be one of low rank, and after keeping us waiting for some time, he referred us to his superiors in office.

Upon hearing this and finding that it was their purpose to turn us out again into the crowded streets, we positively refused to move a single step and insisted on chairs being brought. After some objection, this was done; we seated ourselves in them, and they carried us. On the road, we felt so glad of the rest which the chairs afforded us and thankful at having been able to preach Jesus in spite of Satan's malice. Our joy was evident on our countenances, and as we passed along, we heard some say that we did not look like bad men, while others seemed to pity us. When we arrived at the magistrate's office, I wondered where we were being taken, for though we passed through some great gates that looked like those of the city wall, we were still within the city. A second pair of gates suggested the idea that it was a prison into which we were being carried, but when we came in sight of a large tablet with the inscription *Ming chï fu mu* ("the father and mother of the people"), we felt that we had been conveyed to the right place. This was the title assumed by the mandarins.

Our cards were again sent in, and after a short delay, we were taken into the presence of Ch'en Ta Lao-ie (the Great Venerable Father Ch'en) who, as it proved, had formerly been Tao-tai of Shanghai. Consequently, he knew the importance of treating foreigners with courtesy. Coming before him, some of the people fell on their knees and bowed down to the ground, and my abductor motioned for me to do the same but without success. This mandarin, who seemed to be the highest authority of Tung Chau, wore an opaque blue button on his cap. He came out to meet us and treated us with every possible token of respect. He took us to an inner apartment, a more private room, but we were followed by a large number of writers, runners, and other semi-officials. I related the purpose of our visit and begged permission to give him copies of our books and tracts, for which he thanked me. As I handed him a copy of the New Testament with part of the Old (from Genesis to Ruth) and some tracts, I tried to explain a little about them and give him a brief summary of our teachings. He listened very attentively, as did all the others who were present. He then ordered some refreshments to be brought in, which were very welcome, and he partook of them with us.

After a long stay, we asked permission to see some of the city and distribute the books we had brought, before we left. He kindly consented to this. We mentioned that we had been treated disrespectfully as we came in, but we did not attach much importance to that, because the soldiers knew no better. Not desiring, however, to have such an experience repeated, we requested him to give orders that we were not to be further molested. He promised to do this also, and with every possible token of respect, he accompanied us to the door of his official

residence, sending several runners to see that we were respect-
fully treated. We distributed our books quickly and left the city
quite in state. It was amusing to us to see the way in which the
runners made use of their tails. When the street was blocked
by the crowd, they turned them into whips and laid them about
the people's shoulders to right and left!

We had a little trouble finding our wheelbarrows, but eventu-
ally succeeding, we paid the chair coolies, mounted our humble
vehicles, and returned to the river, accompanied for half the
distance by an attendant from the magistrate's office. Early in
the evening, we got back to the boats in safety, sincerely thankful to our heavenly Father for His gracious protection and aid.

CHAPTER 11

With the Rev. William Burns

After the retaking of Shanghai by the Imperialists in February 1855, I was able to rent a house within the walls of the native city and gladly availed myself of this opportunity to reside among the crowded population left to inhabit the ruins that had survived the war. I made my headquarters here, though often absent on more or less prolonged travels.

At the suggestion of the Rev. Dr. Medhurst, the veteran leader of the London Mission, I adopted the native costume in preference to foreign dress to facilitate travel and residence inland. The Chinese had permitted a foreign firm to build a silk factory some distance inland on the condition that the style of building would be purely Chinese with nothing external to suggest that it was foreign. Much benefit resulted from this change of costume, and I, with most of those associated with me, have continued to use native dress.

The Tai Ping rebellion, which began in 1851, had reached the height of its fleeting success. The great city of Nanking had fallen before the invading host, and within two hundred miles of Shanghai, the rebels had established their headquarters and proceeded to fortify themselves for further conquests. During the summer of 1855, various attempts were made to visit the leaders of the movement to bring some decidedly Christian influence upon them, but so little success was experienced that these efforts were abandoned.

I, among others, had sought to reach Nanking, but finding it impossible, I turned my attention to evangelistic work on the island of Tsung-ming. After some time, I was able to overcome the prejudice and fears of the people such that I could rent a little house and settle down in their midst. This was a great joy and encouragement to me. But before many weeks were over, the local authorities made complaints to the British Consul, who compelled me to move, even though the French Consul had secured a property for the Roman Catholic missionaries within three or four miles of the house I had to vacate. Sorely tried and disappointed by this unexpected hindrance, I reluctantly returned to Shanghai, dreaming little of the blessing that God had in store for me there.

A few months previously, the Rev. William Burns of the English Presbyterian Mission had arrived in that port on his return journey from home. Before proceeding to his former locality of service in the southern province of Fu-kien, like me he had endeavored to visit the Tai Ping rebels at Nanking. Failing in this attempt, he made his headquarters in Shanghai for a season, devoting himself to the evangelization of the surrounding populated regions. Thus, in the autumn of the year, I was providentially led to join with this beloved and honored servant of God.

We journeyed together, evangelizing cities and towns in southern Kiang-su and north Cheh-kiang. We lived in our boats and followed the course of the canals and rivers, which spread like a network over the whole face of the rich and fertile country. Mr. Burns at that time was wearing English dress, but he saw that even though I was the younger and in every way less experienced, I had the quiet listeners. He was followed by the rude boys and by the curious but careless. I was invited to the homes of the people, while he received an apology because of the crowd that would follow his being invited. After some weeks of observation, he also adopted the native dress and enjoyed the increased opportunities that it gave.

Those happy months were an unspeakable joy and privilege to me. His love for the Word was delightful, and his holy, reverential life and constant communing with God made fellowship with him satisfying to the deep cravings of my heart. His accounts of revival work and of persecutions in Canada and Dublin and in Southern China were most instructive, as well as interesting. With true spiritual insight, he often pointed out God's purposes in trials in a way that made all life assume quite a new meaning and value. Especially his views about evangelism as the great work of the church and the order of lay evangelists as a lost order that Scripture required to be restored were seed thoughts, which proved fruitful in the subsequent organization of the China Inland Mission.

Externally, however, our path was not always a smooth one, but when we were permitted to stay for any length of time in a town or city, the opportunity was well utilized. After prayer for blessing, we were in the habit of leaving our boats at about nine o'clock in the morning with a light bamboo stool in hand. Selecting a suitable station, one would mount the stool and speak for twenty minutes, while the other was pleading for blessing. Then, we changed places, and the voice of the first speaker had a rest. After an hour or two, we would move on to another point at some distance from the first and speak again. Usually about midday, we returned to our boats for dinner, fellowship, and prayer, and then we resumed our outdoor work until dusk. After tea and further rest, we would go with our native helpers to some tea shop, where several hours might be spent in free conversation with the people. Not infrequently before leaving a town, we had good reason to believe that much truth had been understood, and we placed many Scriptures and books in the hands of those interested. The following letter was written by Mr. Burns to his mother at home in Scotland about this time:

January 26th, 1856

Taking advantage of a rainy day, which confines me
to my boat, I pen a few lines in addition to a letter
to Dundee, containing particulars which I need not
repeat. It is now forty-one days since I left Shanghai
on this last occasion. A young English missionary, Mr.
Taylor, of the Chinese Evangelization Society, has been
my companion during these weeks – he in his boat, and
I in mine – and we have experienced much mercy and
on some occasions considerable assistance in our work.

I must once more tell the story I have had to tell already
more than once – how four weeks ago on December 29,
I put on the Chinese dress, which I am now wearing.
Mr. Taylor had made this change a few months before,
and I found that he was so much less hindered by the
crowd in his preaching that I concluded it was my duty
to follow his example. We were at that time more than
twice the distance from Shanghai that we are now.
We would still have been at that great distance had we
not met with a band of lawless people, who demanded
money and threatened to break our boats if their
demands were refused. The boatmen were very alarmed
and insisted on returning to some place nearer home.
These violent people had previously broken in a part of
Mr. Taylor's boat, because he did not comply with their
unreasonable demand for books.

We have a large, very large, field of labor in this region,
though it might be difficult presently for one to estab-
lish himself in any particular place; the people listen
with attention, but we need the Power from on High to
convince and convert. Is there any spirit of prayer on
our behalf among God's people in Kilsyth? Or is there

any effort to seek this spirit? How great the need is, and how great the arguments and motives for prayer in this case. The harvest here is indeed great, and the laborers are few and imperfectly fitted without much grace for such a work. And yet grace can make the few and feeble instruments the means of accomplishing great things – things greater than we can even conceive.

The incident referred to in this letter, which led to our return to Shanghai more speedily than we had at first intended, took place on the northern border of Cheh-kiang. We had reached a busy market town known by the name of Wu-chen, or Black Town. We had been told the inhabitants were the wildest and most lawless people in that part of the country. Such indeed we found them to be: the town was a refuge for salt smugglers and other bad characters. The following excerpts are taken from my journal, written at the time:

January 8th, 1856

Commenced our work in Wu-chen this morning by distributing a large number of tracts and some Testaments. The people seemed very surprised, and we could not learn that any foreigner had been here before. We preached twice – once in the temple of the god of War and afterwards in an empty space left by a fire, which had destroyed many houses. In the afternoon, we preached to a large and attentive audience on the same site. In the evening, we adjourned to a tea shop, where we had a good opportunity of speaking until word got out that we were there. When too many people came in, we were obliged to leave. Our native assistants, Tsien and Kuei-hua, were able, however, to remain. Returning to our boats, we spoke to a number of people standing on a bridge and felt we had abundant reason to be thankful and encouraged by the result of our first day's labor.

January 10th, 1856

First we sent Tsien and Kuei-hua to distribute some sheet tracts. After they returned, we went with them, and in a space that had been cleared by fire, we separated and addressed two audiences. On our return to the boats for lunch, we found people waiting, as usual, and desiring books. Some were distributed to those who were able to read them. Then asking them kindly to excuse us while we took our midday meal, I went into my boat and shut the door.

There was hardly time to pour a cup of tea when a battering began, and the roof was at once broken in. I went out at the back and found four or five men taking the large lumps of frozen earth turned up in a field close by – weighing, I should suppose, from seven to fourteen pounds each – and throwing them at the boat. Protesting did not help, and it was not long before a considerable part of the upper structure of the boat was broken to pieces, and a quantity of earth covered the things inside. Finally, Tsien got a boat that was passing to land him a short distance away, and with a few tracts he drew the attention of the men away, thus ending the assault.

We learned that only two of those who had done the mischief were natives of the place; the others were salt smugglers, and the cause of the assault was our not satisfying their unreasonable demand for books. Most providentially, no one was injured. As soon as quiet was somewhat restored, we all met in Mr. Burns's boat and joined in thanksgiving that we had been preserved from personal harm, praying also for the perpetrators of the mischief, and that this incident might be overruled for good to us and to those with us. We then took our lunch and went on shore, and a few steps from the boats we addressed a large multitude that soon assembled. We were specially assisted; we had never been heard with more attention, and not one voice sympathized with the men who had molested us. In the evening at the tea shops, the same spirit was manifested, and some seemed to hear with joy the good news of salvation through a crucified and risen Savior.

As we came home, we passed a barber's shop that was still open, and I went in. While getting my head shaved, I had an opportunity of speaking to a few people and afterwards pasted a couple of sheet tracts on the wall for the benefit of future customers.

January 11th, 1856

A respectable shopkeeper of the name of Yao, who on the first or second day of our stay at Wu-chen had received portions of the New Testament and a tract, came yesterday, when our boat was broken, to beg for some more books. At that time, we were all in confusion from the damage done and from the earth thrown into the boat, so we invited him to come again in a day or two, when we would gladly supply him. This morning he appeared and handed in the following note:

On a former day, I begged Burns and Taylor, the two *Rabbis*, to give me good books. It happened that those of our town whose hearts were deceived by *Satan*, not knowing the *Son of David*, went so far as to dare to *raca* and *moreh* and injure your respected boat at that time. I thank you for promising to give the books later and beg the following: Complete New Testament, Discourse of a Good Man when near his Death, Important Christian Doctrines, an Almanac, Principles of Christianity, Way to make the World Happy – one copy of each. Sung and Tsien and all teachers, I hope are well. Further compliments are unwritten.

This note is interesting, as it showed that he had been reading the New Testament attentively. The italicized words were all taken from it. His use of *raca* and *moreh* for reviling shows their meaning was not lost upon him.

After supplying this man, we went out with Tsien and Kuei-hua to the east of the town and spoke in the street for a short time. Upon returning to the boats, two Chih-li men, who are in the magistrate's office here, visited me. I was helped in speaking to them of a crucified Savior in the Mandarin dialect. Though one of them did not pay much attention, the other did, and he made inquiries that showed the interest he was feeling. When they had left, I went on shore and spoke to the people collected there to whom Kuei-hua had been preaching. The setting sun afforded a parable and reminded one of the words of Jesus, *the night cometh, when no man can work*; as I spoke of the uncertain duration of this life and of our ignorance as to the time of Christ's return, a degree of deep seriousness prevailed that I had never previously witnessed in China. I prayed, and the greatest decorum was observed. I then returned to my boat with a Buddhist priest who had been in the audience, and he admitted that Buddhism was a system of deceit that could give no hope in death.

January 12th, 1856

In the afternoon, we addressed the people on shore close to our boats and in one of the streets of the city and in a tea shop. We distributed books on each occasion. In the evening, we went as usual to speak in the tea shops but determined to go to the opposite end of the town to allow those who lived there a better opportunity of meeting with us. It was a long, straggling place, nearly two English miles in length. As Mr. Burns and I were accustomed to talk together in Chinese, this conclusion was known to those in the boats.

After we had proceeded a short distance, we changed our minds and went instead to the usual tea shop, thinking that people might have gone there expecting to meet us. But this was not the case. We did not find such serious listeners as we had on previous occasions. On this account, Mr. Burns proposed leaving earlier than usual, and we did, telling Tsien and Kuei-hua that they might remain a little longer. Returning to the boats, we gave away a few books, but we were left to go alone with no one accompanying us, as is generally the case. Instead of being a clear night as when we started, we found that it had become intensely dark. On our way, we met the boatman, whose manner seemed very strange, and without giving us any explanation, he blew out the candle of our lantern. We relit the lantern, telling him not to put it out again. To our surprise, he deliberately removed the candle and threw it into the canal. He then walked down along a low wall jutting out to the river's edge and gazed into the water.

Not knowing what was the matter with him, I ran forward to stop him, fearful lest he were going to drown himself, but to my great relief he came quietly back. In answer to our repeated questions, he told us not to speak, for some bad men were seeking to destroy the boats, and they had moved away to avoid them. He then led us to the place where one of them was lying. Before long Tsien and Kuei-hua came and got safely on board, and soon we were joined by the teacher Sung, and the boat moved away.

The cause of all this disturbance was then explained. A man professing to be the constable had come to the boats in our absence with a written demand for ten dollars and a quantity of opium. He stated that there were more than fifty country people (salt smugglers) awaiting our reply in an adjoining tea shop. If we gave them what they wanted and three hundred cash to pay for their tea, we might remain in peace. But if not, they would come at once and destroy our boats. Sung told them that we could not comply with their demand, for we were not engaged in trade, only in preaching and book distribution. We did not have an atom of opium, and our money was nearly all spent. The man, however, told him plainly that he did not believe him, and Sung had no alternative but to seek us out, desiring the man to wait for our reply. Not knowing that we had changed our plans, he sought us in the wrong direction and, of course, in vain.

In the meantime, our boatmen had succeeded in moving off. They were very alarmed; having recently encountered what these men would do in open daylight, they felt no desire to experience what they might attempt by night. Moving away, therefore, they had separated, so if one boat should be injured, the other might afford us a refuge. It was after this that we had met the boatman and had been safely led on board. As Sung repassed the place where we were previously moored, he saw between the trees a dozen or more men and heard them inquiring where the boats had gone, but no one could tell. Fortunately, they sought in vain.

After a while the two boats joined and rowed together for some time. It was already late, and to travel by night in that part of the country was not the way to avoid danger from evil men, so the question arose as to what should be done. We left this for the boatmen to decide; they had moved off on their own accord, and we felt that whatever we personally might desire, we could not compel others to remain in a position of danger on our account. We urged them, however, to quickly do whatever they intended to do, as the next day was the Lord's Day, when we should not wish to travel. We also informed them that wherever we were we must fulfil our mission and preach the gospel. Therefore, it made little difference where we might stay, for even if we passed the night unperceived, we were sure to be found out on the following morning. The men consequently concluded that we might as well return to the place from which we had started. We fully agreed to this, and they turned back accordingly. But – whether by accident or not, we could not tell – they got into another stream and rowed for some time not knowing where they were going. At last, as it was very dark, they moored for the night.

We then called all the boatmen together, with our native assistants, and read to them the ninety-first psalm. It may be imagined how appropriate to our position and need and how sweetly consoling this portion of God's Word was to us:

> *He that dwelleth in the secret place of the most High shall abide under the shadow of the Almighty. I will say of the LORD, He is my refuge and my fortress: My God; in him will I trust. Surely he shall deliver thee from the snare of the fowler, and from the noisome pestilence. He shall cover thee with his feathers, and under his wings shalt thou trust: his truth shall be thy shield and buckler. Thou shalt not be afraid for the terror by night; nor for the arrow that flieth by day; Because he hath set his love upon me, therefore will I deliver him: I will set him on high, because he hath known my name. He shall call upon me, and I will answer him: I will be with him in trouble; I will deliver him, and honour him. With long life will I satisfy him, and shew him my salvation. (Psalm 91:1-5, 14-16)*

We committed ourselves in prayer to His care and keeping. He had covered us with thick darkness and permitted us to escape from the hand of the violent; we retired for the night. Thanks to the kind protection of the Watchman of Israel, who neither slumbers nor forgets His people, we passed in peace and quietness and were enabled, in some measure, to realize the truth of that precious Word: *Thou art my hiding-place and my shield.*

Sunday, January 13th, 1856

This morning I was awakened about four o'clock by violent pain in the knee joint. I had bruised it the day before, and severe inflammation was the result. To my great surprise, I heard the rain pouring down in torrents; the weather had been particularly fine previously. On looking out, we found ourselves so near our former stopping place that, had nothing happened to prevent it, we should not have felt justified in not going into the town to preach as usual; but the rain was so heavy all day that no one could leave the boats. Thus, we enjoyed a delightful day of rest, such as we had not had for some time, and the weather prevented much inquiry being made for us. Had the day been fine, we would most likely have been discovered, even if we had not left the boats. As it was, we were allowed to think in peace with wonder and gratitude of the gracious dealings of our God, who had led us apart into "a desert place" to rest awhile.

Monday, January 14th, 1856

A cloudless morning. Before daybreak, one of the native assistants went to get some clothes, which had been given out for washing. He came back with news that, in spite of the drenching rain yesterday, men had been seeking us in all directions. We had been kept in peace and safety, however, *under the shadow of the Almighty.*

The boatmen were so thoroughly alarmed that they would stay no longer and moved off at dawn. Because of my lameness, I was confined to my quarters and had no alternative but to go with them. In the afternoon, we reached Ping-wang on the way to Shanghai.

> Ill that God blesses is our good,
> And unblest good is ill;
> And all is right that seems most wrong,
> If it be His sweet will.

East gate and sentry box, Bhamô, Burmah

CHAPTER 12

Called to Swatow

Having to leave the neighborhood of Black Town unexpectedly was a real disappointment to us, as we had hoped to spend some time evangelizing in that district. We were to prove, however, that no unforeseen mischance had happened, but that these circumstances, which seemed so trying, were necessary links in the chain of a divinely ordered providence, guiding us to other and wider spheres.

God does not permit persecution to arise without sufficient reason. . . . He was leading us by a way that we did not know, but it was His way nonetheless.

> O Lord! how happy should we be,
> If we could leave our cares to Thee,
>   If we from self could rest;
> And feel at heart that One above,
> In perfect wisdom, perfect love,
>   Is working for the best.

When we reached Shanghai, we thought we could return inland in a few days with fresh supplies of books and money. We met a Christian captain who had been trading at Swatow, and he described to us the great need of that region. He explained how the British merchants living on Double Island were selling opium and engaging in the coolie trade (practically a slave traffic), while there was no British missionary to preach the gospel. The Spirit of God impressed me with the feeling that this was

His call, but for days I felt that I could not obey it. I had never had such a spiritual father as Mr. Burns; I had never known such holy, happy fellowship. I said to myself that it could not be God's will that we should separate.

In great unrest of soul, I went one evening with Mr. Burns to take tea at the house of the Rev. R. Lowrie of the American Presbyterian Mission at the South Gate of Shanghai. After tea, Mrs. Lowrie played for us *The Missionary Call*. I had never heard it before, and it greatly affected me. My heart was almost broken before it was finished, and I said to the Lord in the words that had been sung:

And I will go!
I may no longer doubt to give up friends, and idol hopes,
And every tie that binds my heart. . . .
Henceforth, then, it matters not, if storm or sunshine be
    my earthly lot, bitter or sweet my cup;
I only pray, God, make me holy,
And my spirit nerve for the stern hour of strife.

Upon leaving, I asked Mr. Burns to come home with me to the little house that was still my headquarters in the native city. With many tears, I told him how the Lord had been leading me and how rebellious I had been and unwilling to leave him for this new sphere of labor. He listened with a strange look of surprise and pleasure rather than pain, and he answered that he had determined that very night to tell me that he had heard the Lord's call to Swatow, and his one regret had been the prospect of the severance of our happy fellowship. So we went together and reestablished missionary work in that part of China, which in later years has been so abundantly blessed.

Long before this time, the Rev. R. Lechler of the Basel Missionary Society had roamed widely in the neighborhood of

Swatow and the surrounding regions. Driven about from place to place, he had done work that was not forgotten, although ultimately he was obliged to retire to Hong Kong. For more than forty years, this earnest-hearted servant of God has continued in "labors more abundant." Quite recently he has left Hong Kong with his devoted wife to return again inland and spend the strength of his remaining years among the people he has so long and truly loved.

Captain Bowers, the Christian friend who had been used of God in bringing the needs of Swatow before Mr. Burns and me, was overjoyed when he heard of our decision to devote ourselves to the evangelization of that busy, important, and populous commercial center. Since he was about to sail back on his return journey, he gladly offered us free passages on board the *Geelong*, in which we left Shanghai early in the month of March 1856.

A favorable journey of six days brought us to Double Island, where we landed in the midst of a small but very ungodly community of foreigners, who were engaged in the opium trade and other commercial enterprises. Unwilling to be identified with these fellow countrymen, we were most desirous of obtaining quarters at once within the native city, which was situated on a promontory of the mainland, five miles farther up at the mouth of the Han River. We experienced great difficulty in this attempt to obtain a footing among the people. Indeed, it seemed as though we should fail altogether, and we were helplessly cast upon the Lord in prayer. Our God soon undertook for us. Meeting one day with a Cantonese merchant, a relative of the highest official in the town, Mr. Burns addressed him in the Cantonese dialect. This gentleman was so pleased at being spoken to by a foreigner in his own tongue that he became our friend and secured us a lodging. We had only one little room, however, and I shall not easily forget the long, hot summer months in that oven-like place, where towards the eaves one could touch the heated tiles with one's hand. It was impossible to obtain more room or better accommodations.

We varied our stay by visits to the surrounding country, but the difficulties and dangers that encountered us were so great and constant that our former work in the North began to appear safe and easy in comparison. The hatred and contempt of the Cantonese was very painful; "foreign devil," "foreign dog," or "foreign pig" were the most common names they called us. All of this led us into deeper fellowship, though, than I had ever known before with Him who was *despised and rejected of men*.

In our visits to the countryside, we were in peril of being seized at any time and held for ransom. The people commonly declared that the whole district was "without emperor, without ruler, and without law." Certainly, might was right in those days. On one occasion, we were visiting a small town and found that the inhabitants had captured a wealthy man of another clan. A large ransom was demanded for his release, and on his refusing to pay it, they had smashed his ankle bones, one by one, with a club and, thus, extorted the promise they desired. There was nothing but God's protection to prevent our being treated in the same way. The towns were all walled, and one such place would contain ten or twenty thousand people of the same clan and surname, who were frequently at war with the people living in the next town. To be kindly received in one place was not uncommonly a source of danger in the next. In circumstances such as these, God often manifested His preserving care.

After a time the local mandarin became ill, and the native doctors were unable to relieve him. He had heard of acquired benefit from some who had been under my treatment and was led to seek our help. God blessed the medicines we gave, and grateful for relief, he advised our renting a house for a hospital and dispensary. Having his permission, we were able to secure the entire premises, one room of which we had previously occupied. I had left my stock of medicine and surgical instruments under the care of my friend, the late Mr. Wylie, in Shanghai, so I went back at once to fetch them.

Mr. Burns came down from a town called Am-po that we had visited together several times to see me off, and he returned again after I had sailed with two native evangelists sent up from Hong Kong by the Rev. J. Johnson of the American Baptist Missionary Union. The people were willing to listen to their preaching and accept their books as a gift, but they would not buy them. One night robbers broke in and carried off everything they had, with the exception of their stock of literature, which was supposed to be valueless. Very early the next morning, they were visited by persons wishing to buy books, and the sales continued. By breakfast time, they had cash enough to procure food and also pay for the passage of one of the men to Double Island, below Swatow, with a letter to Mr. Burns's agent to supply him with money. Purchasers continued coming during that day and the next, and our friends lacked nothing. On the third day, they could not sell a single book. Then, however, when the cash from their sales was just exhausted, the messenger returned with supplies.

It was early in July, after about four months' residence in Swatow, that I left for Shanghai, intending to return in the course of a few weeks with my medical apparatus, for further work in association with the Rev. William Burns. A new and promising field seemed to be opening before us, and it was with much hopeful anticipation that we looked forward to the future of the work. Marked blessing was indeed in store for the city and neighborhood of Swatow; but it was not the purpose of God that either of us should remain to reap the harvest. While in the interior, Mr. Burns was taken up and imprisoned by the Chinese authorities soon after I left. He was then sent to Canton. And though he returned to Swatow after the war broke out, he was called away for other service, which prevented his subsequent return. My journey to Shanghai proved to be the first step in a diverging pathway leading to other spheres.

"THE MISSIONARY CALL"

CHORUS FOR LAST VERSE.

Through a - ges of e - ter - nal years, My spi - rit nev - er shall re-
Through a - ges of e - ter - nal years, My spi - rit nev - er shall re-

- pent, that toil and suf - f'ring once were mine.... be - low.
- pent, that toil and suf - f'ring once were mine.... be - low.

2. Why live I here? the vows of God are | on me; | and I may not stop
   to play with shadows or pluck earthly flowers, | till I my work
   have done, and | rendered up ac | count.

3. And I will | go! | I may no longer doubt to give up friends,
   and idol | hopes, | and every tie that binds my heart to |
   thee, my | country.

4. Henceforth, then, it matters not, if storm or sunshine be
   my | earthly lot, | bitter or sweet my | cup; | I only pray:
   "God make me holy, and my spirit nerve for the stern |
   hour of strife!"

5. And when one for whom Satan hath struggled as he hath for
   | me, | has gained at last that blessed | shore, | Oh! how
   this heart will glow with | gratitude and | love.

CHAPTER 13

Man Proposes, God Disposes

I t is interesting to notice the various events, which in the providence of God united in preventing my return to Swatow and ultimately led to my settling in Ningpo, and making that the center for the development of future labors.

Upon reaching Shanghai, I was greatly dismayed to find that the premises in which my medicines and instruments had been stored were burned down, and all the medicines and many of the instruments were destroyed. This appeared to be a great calamity to me, and I fear I was more disposed with faithless Jacob to say, *all these things are against me*, than to recognize that *all things work together for good*. I had not learned to think of God as the One Great Circumstance *in [whom] we live, and move, and have our being;* and of *all* lesser, external circumstances, as the kindest, wisest, and best, because they are either ordered or permitted by Him. Hence, my disappointment and trial were very great.

Medicines were expensive in Shanghai, and my means were limited. I therefore set out on an inland journey to Ningpo, hoping to obtain a supply from Dr. William Parker, also a member of the Chinese Evangelization Society. I took my few remaining possessions, the principal being my watch, a few surgical instruments, a concertina, and books for the study of Chinese, which in those days were very expensive, but I left behind in Shanghai a portion of my money.

The country through which I had to pass was suffering much from drought. It was the height of summer, and the water in the Grand Canal was very low, having been largely drawn upon for the neighboring rice fields, as the water also evaporated from the intense heat. I had determined to make the journey as much of a mission tour as possible and set out well supplied with Christian tracts and books. After fourteen days traveling slowly through the populated country, preaching and distributing books, we reached a large town called Shih-mun-wan. I exhausted my supply of literature, so I decided not to linger over the rest of the journey but to reach Ningpo as speedily as possible via the city of Hai-ning.

August 4th, 1856

There was no water beyond Shih-mun-wan, so I paid off my boat, hired coolies to carry my things as far as Chang'an, and before sunrise, we were on the way. I walked on alone, leaving my servant to follow with the men, who made frequent stops to rest. On reaching a city through which we had to pass, I waited for them in a tea shop just outside the North Gate. The coolies came very slowly and seemed tired when they arrived. I soon found that they were both opium smokers, so although they had only carried a load that one strong man would think nothing of taking three times the distance, they really seemed wearied.

After some rice and tea and an hour's rest – including, I have no doubt, a smoke of the opium pipe – they were a little refreshed, and I proposed moving on that we might get to Chang'an before the sun became too powerful. My servant, however, had a friend in the city, and he desired to spend the day there and go on the next morning. But I objected to this, wishing to reach Hai-ning that night if possible. We therefore set off, entered the North Gate, and passed through about a third of the city, when the coolies stopped to rest. They said they were not able to carry the burden on to Chang'an. Finally, they agreed to take it to the South Gate, where they were to be paid in proportion to the distance they had carried it. The servant undertook to call other coolies and go along with them.

I walked on as in the first instance. Because the distance was only about four miles, I soon reached Chang'an and waited their arrival. Meanwhile, I engaged coolies for the rest of the journey to Hai-ning. Having waited a long time, I began to wonder at the delay, and at length it became too late to finish the journey to Hai-ning that night. I felt somewhat annoyed. Except that my feet were blistered and the afternoon very hot, I should have gone back to meet them and urge them on. At last, I concluded that my servant must have gone to his friend's and would not appear until evening. But evening came, and still there was no sign of them.

Feeling very uneasy, I began to inquire whether they had been seen. At last, a man responded, "Are you a guest from Shih-mun-wan?" I answered in the affirmative.

"Are you going to Hai-ning?"

"That is my destination."

"Then your things have gone on before you, for I was sitting in a tea shop when a coolie came in, took a cup of tea, and set off for Hai-ning in a great hurry, saying that the bamboo box and bed he carried, which were such as you describe yours to have been, were from Shih-mun-wan. He had to take them to Hai-ning tonight, where he was to be paid at the rate of ten cash a pound." From this, I concluded that my goods went on before me, but it was impossible to follow them at once, for I was too tired to walk, and it was already dark.

Under these circumstances, all I could do was to seek lodging for the night, and it was no easy task to find it. After raising my heart to God to ask His aid, I walked through to the farther end of the town, where I thought the news of a foreigner's being in the place might not have spread and looked for an inn. I soon came to one and went in, hoping that I might pass unquestioned, as it was already dark. Asking for the menu, I was told that cold rice – which proved to be more than "rather burnt" – and snakes, fried in lamp oil, were all that could be had. Not wishing any question to be raised as to my nationality, I was compelled to order some and tried to make a meal, but with little success.

While thus engaged, I said to the landlord, "I suppose I can arrange to spend the night here?"

He replied in the affirmative, but bringing out his book, he added: "In these unsettled times, we are required by the authorities to keep a record of our lodgers: may I ask your respected family name?"

"My unworthy family name is Tai," I responded.

"And your honorable second name?"

"My humble name is Ia-koh" (James).

"What an extraordinary name! I never heard it before. How do you write it?"

I told him and added, "It is a common name in the district from which I come."

"And may I ask whence you come and whither you are going?"

"I am journeying from Shanghai to Ningpo by way of Hangzhou."

"What may be your honorable profession?"

"I heal the sick."

"Oh! You are a physician," the landlord remarked, and to my intense relief, he closed the book. His wife, however, took up the conversation.

"You are a physician, are you?" said she. "I am glad of that, for I have a daughter afflicted with leprosy. If you will cure her, you shall have your supper and bed for nothing."

I was curious enough to inquire what my supper and bed were to cost, if paid for, and to my amusement, I found they were worth less than three halfpence of our money!

Being unable to benefit the girl, I declined to prescribe for her, saying that leprosy was a very stubborn disease, and I had no medicines with me.

The mother, however, brought pen and paper, urging, "You can at least write a prescription, which will do no harm, if it does no good."

But this also I declined to do and requested to be shown my bed. I was conducted to a very miserable room on the ground floor where, on some boards raised upon two stools, I passed the night without bed or pillow except my umbrella and shoes and without any mosquito netting. Ten or eleven other lodgers were sleeping in the same room, so I could not take anything off for fear of its being stolen. I found I was by no means too warm as midnight came on.

August 5th, 1856

As may be supposed, I arose but little rested or refreshed and felt far from well. I had to wait a long time before breakfast could be obtained, and then there was another delay before I could get change for the only dollar I had with me, because it was chipped in one or two places. More than three hundred cash were deducted from its value on this account, which was a serious loss to me in my tenuous position.

I then sought for news of my servant and coolies throughout the town, as I thought it possible that they might have arrived later or come in the morning. The town is large, long, and straggling, being nearly two miles from one end to the other, so this occupied some time. I gained no information, however. Footsore and weary, I set out for Hai-ning in the full heat of the day. The journey – about eight miles – took me a long time, but a village halfway afforded a resting place and a cup of tea, both of which I gladly availed myself of. When I was about to leave, a heavy shower of rain descended, and the delay gave me time to speak a little to the people about the truths of the gospel.

The afternoon was far spent before I approached the northern suburb of Hai-ning, where I began inquiries, but I heard no news of my servant or things. I was told that outside the East Gate I might be more likely to hear of them, as it was there the sea-junks called. I therefore proceeded and sought them outside the Little East Gate, but in vain. Very weary, I sat down in a tea shop to rest. A number of persons from one of the mandarin's offices came in and made inquiries as to who I was and where I had come from. Realizing the purpose of my search, one of the men in the tea shop said, "A bamboo box and a bed, such as you describe, were carried past here about half an hour ago. The bearer seemed to be going towards either the Great East Gate or the South Gate; you had better go to the rooms there and inquire." I asked him to accompany me in the search and promised to reward him for his trouble, but he would not. Another man offered to go with me, so we set off together and made diligent inquiries both inside and outside the two gates, but all in vain. I then engaged a man to make a thorough search, promising him a liberal reward if he should be successful. In the meantime, I had some dinner and addressed a large concourse of people who had gathered.

When he returned, having met with no success, I said to him, "I am now quite exhausted. Will you help me find quarters for the night, and then I will pay you for your trouble?" He was willing to befriend me, and we set off in search of lodgings. At the first place or two, the people would not receive me. When we first went in, they seemed willing to accommodate me, but the presence of a man who followed us seemed to alarm them, and I was refused. I discovered he was associated with one of the government offices. We went to a third place, and no longer followed by the mandarin's messenger, we were promised quarters; some tea was brought, and I paid the man who had accompanied me for his trouble.

Soon after he was gone, some official people came. They soon went away, but I was then told I could not stay there that night. A young man blamed them for their heartless behavior and said, "Never mind, come with me; and if we cannot get better lodgings for you, you shall sleep at our house."

I went with him, but we found the people of his house unwilling to receive me. Weary and footsore, so that I could scarcely stand, I had to seek quarters again and at last got a promise of them. However, a little crowd was gathering by the door; they asked me to go to a tea shop and wait there until the people had retired, or they would be unable to accommodate me. There was no help for it, so I went, still accompanied by the young man, and waited until past midnight. Then we left for the promised resting place; but my guide could not find it, and he led me about to another part of the city. Finally, between one and two o'clock, he left me to pass the rest of the night as best I could.

I was opposite a temple, but it was closed; so I lay down on the stone steps in front of it. Putting my money under my head for a pillow, I would have soon been asleep in spite of the cold had I not perceived a person coming stealthily towards me. As he approached, I saw he was one of the beggars so common in China, and I had no doubt his intention was to rob me of my money. I did not stir but watched his movements and prayed to my Father not to leave me in this hour of trial. The man came up, looked at me for some time to assure himself that I was asleep (it was so dark that he could not see my eyes fixed on him), and then began to feel about me gently. I said to him in the quietest tone, to convince him that I was not, nor had been, sleeping, "What do you want?" He made no answer but went away.

I was very thankful to see him go, and when he was out

of sight, I put as much of my cash that would not go into my pocket safely up my sleeve, and I made my pillow of a stone projection of the wall. It was not long before I began to doze, but I was aroused by the all-but-noiseless footsteps of two persons approaching, for my nervous system was rendered so sensitive by exhaustion that the slightest noise startled me. Again I sought protection from Him who alone was my stay, and I lay still as before, until one of them came up and began to feel under my head for the cash. I spoke again, and they sat down at my feet. I asked them what they were doing; they replied that they, like me, were going to pass the night there. I then requested them to take the opposite side, as there was plenty of room, and leave this side to me, but they would not move from my feet, so I raised myself up and set my back against the wall.

They said, "You had better lie down and sleep; if you do not, you will be unable to walk to-morrow. Do not be afraid; we shall not leave you and will see that no one hurts you."

"Listen to me," I replied. "I do not want your protection; I need it not; I am not a Chinese; I do not worship your sense-less, helpless idols. I worship God; He is my Father; I trust in Him. I know well what you are and what your intentions are and shall keep my eye on you and shall not sleep."

After this, one of them went away, but he soon returned with a third companion. I felt very uneasy, but looked to God for help. Once or twice one of them got up to see if I was asleep. I only said, "Do not be mistaken; I am not sleeping." Occasionally my head dropped, and this was a signal for one of them to rise, but I at once roused myself and made some remark. As the night slowly passed on, I felt very weary; to keep myself awake, as well as to cheer my mind, I sang several hymns, repeated aloud some portions of Scripture, and engaged in prayer in English, to the great annoyance of my companions, who seemed as if they would have given anything to get me to desist. After that, they troubled me no more and shortly before dawn, they left me, and I got a little sleep.

August 6th, 1856

I was awakened by the young man who had so misled me on the previous evening. He was very rude and insisted on my getting up and paying him for his trouble. He even went so far as to try to accomplish by force what he wanted. This roused me, and in an unguarded moment with very improper feeling, I seized his arm with such a grasp that he little expected I was capable of and dared him to lay a finger upon me again or annoy me further. This quite changed his manner; he let me quietly remain until the guns announced the opening of the gates of the city. Then he begged me to give him some money to buy opium with. Needless to say, I refused. I gave him the price of two candles that he said he had burned while with me last night. I learned he was connected with one of the mandarin's offices.

As soon as possible, I bought some rice gruel and tea for breakfast, and then once more I made a personal search for my things. Some hours later with no success, I set out on the return journey, and after a long, weary, and painful walk, I reached Chang'an about noon. Here also, my inquiries failed to give me any trace of the missing goods, so I had a meal cooked in a tea shop, got a thorough wash, and bathed my inflamed feet. After dinner, I rested and slept until four in the afternoon.

Much refreshed, I then set out to return to the city at the South Gate where I had parted with my servant and coolies two days before. On the way, I was led to reflect on the goodness of God and recollected that I had not prayed for lodgings last night. I felt condemned, too, that I should have been so anxious for my few things, while the many precious souls around me had caused so little emotion. I came as a sinner and pleaded the blood of Jesus, realizing that I was accepted in Him – pardoned, cleansed, sanctified – and oh, the love of Jesus, how great I felt it to be! I knew something more than I had ever previously known of what it was to be despised and rejected. I experienced having nowhere to lay my head. I felt more than ever before the greatness of that love which caused Him to leave His home in glory and suffer for me – nay, to lay down His very life upon the cross. I thought of Him as *despised and rejected of men; a man of sorrows, and acquainted with grief*; I thought of Him at Jacob's well, weary, hungry, and thirsty, yet finding it His meat and drink to do His Father's will, and I contrasted this inadequacy of my love. I looked to Him for pardon for the past and for grace and strength to do His will in the future, to tread more closely in His footsteps and be more than ever wholly His. I prayed for myself, for friends in England, and for my brethren in the work. Sweet tears of mingled joy and sorrow flowed freely; the road was almost forgotten, and before I was aware of it, I had reached my destination. Outside the South Gate, I took a cup of tea, asked about my lost luggage, and spoke of the love of Jesus. Then I entered the city, and after many vain inquiries, I left by the North Gate.

I felt so refreshed both in mind and body by the communion I had on my walk to the city that I thought I was able to finish the remaining six miles back to Shih-mun-wan that evening. First, I went into another tea shop to buy some native cakes and was making a meal of them, when who should come in but one of the identical coolies who had carried my things the first stage. From him, I learned that after I left them, they had taken my luggage to the South Gate. Then my servant went away, but when he returned, he said that I had gone on, and he did not intend to start at once but would spend the day with his friend and then rejoin me. They carried the things to this friend's house and left them there. I convinced him to go with me to the house and learned that the man had spent the day and night with them. The next morning he had called other coolies and set off for Hangzhou. This was all I could gather; so, unable to do anything but proceed on my return journey to Shanghai with all expediency, I left the city again. It was now too late to go on to Shih-mun-wan. I looked to my Father to supply all my need and received another token of His ceaseless love and care. I was invited to sleep on a hong boat, which was in the dry bed of the river. The night was very cold and the mosquitoes troublesome. Still, I got a little rest, and at sunrise I was up and continued my journey.

August 7th, 1856

I felt very ill at first and had a sore throat, but I reflected on the wonderful goodness of God who enabled me to bear the heat by day and the cold by night for so long. I felt also that quite a load was taken off my mind. I had committed myself and my affairs to the Lord and knew that if it was for my good and for His glory, my things would be restored; if not, all would be for the best. I hoped that the most trying part of my journey was drawing to a close, and this helped me, weary and footsore, on the way. After I arrived at Shih-mun-wan and ate breakfast, I found I had eight hundred and ten in cash. I knew that the hong boat fare to Kia-hing Fu was one hundred and twenty cash and to Shanghai three hundred and sixty. That left me just three hundred and thirty cash – or twelve pence and a fraction – for three or four days' provisions. I went at once to the boat office, but to my dismay, I found that from the dry state of the river, goods had not come down, so no boat would leave today and perhaps none tomorrow. I inquired if there were any letter boats for Kia-hing Fu; I was told that they had already left. The only remaining resource was to determine if I could get passage on any private boats. My search, however, was in vain; I could get no boat to go all the way to Shanghai or my difficulty would have been at an end.

Just at this time, I saw a letter boat at a turn in the canal that was going in the direction of Kia-hing Fu. I concluded this must be one of the Kia-hing boats that had been unexpectedly detained, and I set off after it as fast as hope and the necessities of the case would carry me. For the time being, weariness and sore feet were both forgotten. After a chase of about a mile, I overtook it.

"Are you going to Kia-hing Fu?" I called out.

"No," was the only answer.

"Are you going in that direction?"

"No."

"Will you give me a passage as far as you do go that way?"

Still "No," and nothing more.

Completely dispirited and exhausted, I sank down on the grass and fainted.

As consciousness returned, some voices reached my ear, and I found they were talking about me. One said, "He speaks pure Shanghai dialect," and from their own speech, I knew them to be Shanghai people. Raising myself, I saw that they were on a large hong boat on the other side of the canal. After a few words, they sent their small boat to fetch me, and I went on board the junk. They were very kind and gave me some tea; when I was refreshed and able to partake of it, they gave me some food also. I then took my shoes and stockings off to ease my feet, and the boatman kindly provided me with hot water to bathe them. When they heard my story and saw the blisters on my feet, they evidently pitied me and hailed every boat that passed to see if it was going my way. Not finding one, by and by, after a few hours' sleep, I went ashore with the captain, intending to preach in the temple of Kwan Ti.

Before leaving the junk, I told the captain and those on

board that I was not able to help myself; I did not have enough strength to walk to Kia-hing Fu. Having been unable to get a passage today, I no longer had sufficient means to take me there by letter boat, which was an expensive mode of traveling. I did not know how the God whom I served would help me, but I had no doubt He would do so, and my business now was to serve Him where I was. I also told them that the help, which I knew would come, should be evidence to them of the truth of the religion, which other missionaries and I had preached at Shanghai.

On our way to the town, while engaged in conversation with the captain, we saw a letter boat coming up. The captain drew my attention to it, but I reminded him that I no longer had the means of paying for my passage on it. He hailed it, nevertheless, and found that it was going to a place about nine English miles from Shanghai; from there one of the boatmen would carry the mail overland to the city. He then said, "This gentleman is a foreigner from Shanghai, who has been robbed, and no longer has the means of returning. If you will take him with you as far as you go and then engage a sedan chair to carry him the rest of the way, he will pay you in Shanghai. You see, my boat is lying aground yonder for want of water and cannot get away. Now, I will stand surety; if this gentleman does not pay when you get to Shanghai, I will do so on your return."

This unsolicited kindness on the part of a Chinaman, a perfect stranger, will appear the more remarkable to anyone acquainted with the character of the Chinese, who are generally most reluctant to risk their money. Those on the letter boat agreed to the terms, and I was taken on board as a passenger. Oh, how thankful I felt for this providential intervention and to be once more on my way to Shanghai!

Letter boats such as the one on which I was now traveling are of a long, narrow build and very limited as to their inside accommodation. One has to lie down all the time they are in motion, as a slight movement would easily upset them. This was no irksome condition to me, however; on the contrary, I was only too glad to be quiet. These are the quickest boats I have seen in China. Each one is worked by two men, who relieve one another continuously night and day. They row with their feet and paddle with their hands; if the wind is quite favorable, they row with their feet and with one hand manage a small sail, while steering with the other.

After a pleasant and speedy journey, I reached Shanghai in safety on August 9, through the help of Him who has said, I will never leave thee, nor forsake thee, and lo, I am with you always, even unto the end of the world.

Teng-yueh, the westernmost walled city in China

CHAPTER 14

Providential Guidance

It now seemed very clear that the lost property – including everything I possessed in China, with the exception of a small sum of money providentially left in Shanghai – had been deliberately stolen by my servant, who had gone off with it to Hangzhou. The first question, of course, was how best to act for the good of the man who had been the cause of so much trouble. It would not have been difficult to take steps that would have led to his punishment, though the likelihood of any reparation being made for the loss sustained was very small. But the consideration, which weighed most heavily on me, was that the thief was a man for whose salvation I had labored and prayed. I felt that to prosecute him would not demonstrate the teaching of the Sermon on the Mount in which we had read together: *Resist not evil*, and other similar precepts. Finally, concluding that his soul was more valuable than the forty pounds worth of things I had lost, I wrote and told him this, reminding him of his need for repentance and faith in the Lord Jesus Christ. The course I took found approval with my Christian friends in England, one of whom was led to send me a check for forty pounds – the first of many received from the same kind helper.

Having obtained the little money left in Shanghai, I set out for Ningpo to seek assistance from Dr. Parker in replacing the medicines I had lost by fire. After accomplishing this, I returned once more to Shanghai, en route for Swatow, hoping to rejoin my much-loved friend Mr. Burns in the work in that important center. God had willed it otherwise, however; the delay caused by the robbery was sufficient to prevent me from starting for the South as I had intended.

Over the political horizon, storm clouds had long been gathering, precursors of coming war; early in October of this year (1856), the affair of the lorcha *Arrow* at Canton led to the commencement of hostilities. Very soon, China was involved in a second prolonged struggle with foreign powers; missionary operations, in the South at any rate, had to be largely suspended. News of these events with letters from Mr. Burns arrived just in time to meet me in Shanghai, as I was leaving for Swatow. Because I was hindered, I could not but realize the hand of God in closing the door I had so desired to enter.

While in Ningpo, I had made the acquaintance of Mr. John Jones, who represented the Chinese Evangelization Society in that city with Dr. Parker. Unable to return to Swatow, I decided to join these brethren in the Ningpo work and set out at once upon the journey. On the afternoon of the second day, we were already about thirty miles from Shanghai. Mr. Jones and I drew near the large and important city of Sung-kiang, and I mentioned going ashore to preach the gospel to the multitudes that lined the banks and crowded the approaches to the city gates.

Among the passengers on board the boat was one intelligent man, who in the course of his travels had been abroad a good deal and had even visited England, where he went by the name of Peter. As might be expected, he had heard something of the gospel but had never experienced its saving power. On the previous evening, I had drawn him into earnest conversation about his salvation. The man listened with attention; he was even moved to tears, but I saw no definite result. I was pleased, therefore, when he asked to be allowed to accompany me and hear me preach.

I went into the cabin of the boat to prepare tracts and books for distribution on landing with my Chinese friend, when suddenly I was startled by a splash and a cry from outside. I sprang on deck and took in the situation at a glance. Peter was gone! The other men were all there, on board, looking helplessly at the spot where he had disappeared, but making no effort to save him. A strong wind was carrying the junk rapidly forward in spite of a steady current in the opposite direction, and the low-lying, shrubless shore afforded no landmark to indicate how far we had left the drowning man behind.

I instantly let down the sail and leapt overboard in the hope of finding him. Unsuccessful, I looked around in agonizing suspense and saw a fishing boat with a peculiar dragnet with hooks close to me, which I knew would bring him up.

"Come!" I cried, as hope revived in my heart. "Come and drag over this spot directly; a man is drowning here!"

"Veh bin" (It is not convenient) was the unfeeling answer.

"Don't talk of *convenience*!" I cried in agony. "A man is drowning, I tell you!"

"We are busy fishing," they responded, "and cannot come."

"Never mind your fishing," I said. "I will give you more money than many a day's fishing will bring; only come – come at once!"

"How much money will you give us?"

"We cannot stay to discuss that now! Come, or it will be too late. I will give you five dollars" (then worth about thirty shillings in English money).

"We won't do it for that," replied the men. "Give us twenty dollars, and we will drag."

"I do not possess so much; do come quickly, and I will give you all I have!"

"How much may that be?"

"I don't know exactly, about fourteen dollars."

At last, but even then slowly enough, they paddled the boat over and let the net down. Less than a minute sufficed to bring up the body of the missing man. The fishermen were clamorous and indignant, because their exorbitant demand was delayed while efforts at resuscitation were being made. But all was in vain – his life was gone.

For me this incident was profoundly sad and full of significance, suggesting a far more mournful reality. Were those fishermen not actually guilty of this poor Chinaman's death, in that they had the means of saving him at hand, if they would have used them? For sure they were guilty. And yet, let us pause before we pronounce judgment against them, lest a greater than Nathan answer: *Thou art the man.* Is it so hard-hearted, so wicked a thing to neglect to save the body? Of how much more severe a punishment then, is he worthy who leaves the soul to perish, who like Cain says, *Am I my brother's keeper?* The Lord Jesus commands, commands *me*, commands *you*, my brother, and *you*, my sister. *Go*, says He. *Go ye into all the world, and preach the gospel to every creature.* Shall we say to *Him*, "No, it is not convenient"? Shall we tell *Him* that we are busy fishing and cannot go? That we have bought a piece of ground and cannot go? That we have purchased five yoke of oxen or have married or are engaged in other and more interesting pursuits and cannot go? Before long *we must all appear before the judgment seat of Christ; that every one may receive the things done in his body.* Let us remember, let us pray for, let us labor for the unevangelized Chinese; or we shall sin against our own souls. Let us consider *Who* it is that has said, *If thou forbear to deliver them that are drawn unto death, and those that are ready to be slain; if thou sayest, Behold, we knew it not; doth not he that pondereth the heart consider it? and he that keepeth thy soul, doth not he know it? and shall not he render to every man according to his works?* (Proverbs 24:11-12)

Through midnight gloom from Macedon
The cry of myriads as of one,
The voiceful silence of despair,
Is eloquent in awful prayer,
The soul's exceeding bitter cry,
"Come o'er and help us, or we die."

How mournfully it echoes on!
For half the earth is Macedon;
These brethren to their brethren call,
And by the Love which loves them all,
And by the whole world's Life they cry,
"O ye that live, behold we die!"

By other sounds the world is won
Than that which wails from Macedon;
The roar of gain is round it rolled,
Or men unto themselves are sold,
And cannot list the alien cry,
"O hear and help us, lest we die!"

Yet with that cry from Macedon
The very car of Christ rolls on;
"I come; who would abide My day,
In yonder wilds prepare My way;
My voice is crying in their cry;
Help ye the dying, lest ye die."

Jesu, for men of Man the Son,
Yea, Thine the cry from Macedon;
O by the kingdom and the power
And glory of Thine advent hour,
Wake heart and will to hear their cry;
Help us to help them, lest we die!

Group of Christians at Lan-k'i, Cheh-kiang

CHAPTER 15

Settlement in Ningpo

The autumn of 1856 was well advanced before I reached Ningpo, one of the most ancient and influential cities on the coast of China. Opened to the residence of foreigners in 1842 by the treaty of Nanking, it had long been the scene of missionary labors. Within its swarming thoroughfares, the busy tide of life runs high. Four hundred thousand human beings dwell within or around the five-mile circuit of its ancient wall, every one a soul that Jesus loves, and for whom He died.

As winter drew on, I rented a native house in Wu-gyiao-deo, or Lake Head Street. It was not a very comfortable residence. I have a very distinct memory of tracing my initials on the snow, which had collected upon my blanket during the night in the large, barn-like upper room, which was subdivided into four or five smaller rooms. Each of these was comfortably ceiled. The tiling of an unceiled Chinese house may keep off the rain, if it happens to be sound, but it does not afford good protection against snow, which will beat up through crannies and crevices and find its way inside. Even though the little house's fittings were unfinished, it was well adapted for work among the people; I thankfully settled down there, finding ample scope for service – morning, noon, and night.

During the latter part of this year, my mind was troubled about continued connection with my Society, because it was frequently in debt. Personally, I had always avoided debt and kept within my salary, though at times only by very careful economy. Now there was no difficulty in doing this, for my income was larger, the country was in a more peaceful state, and things were not so dear. But the Society itself was in debt. The quarterly bills, which we were instructed to submit, were often met by borrowed money, and a correspondence began which terminated in my resigning the following year for honorable reasons.

To me it seemed that the teaching of God's Word was unmistakably clear: *Owe no man any thing.* In my mind, to borrow money implied a contradiction of Scripture, a confession that God had withheld some good thing, and a determination to get for ourselves what He had not given. Could that which was wrong for one Christian to do be right for an association of Christians? Or could any amount of precedents make a wrong course justifiable? If the Word taught me anything, it taught me to have no connection with debt. I could not think that God was poor, that He was short of resources, or unwilling to supply any want of whatever work was really His. It seemed to me that if there were lack of funds to carry on work, then it could not be the work of God to that degree, in that special development, or at that time. To satisfy my conscience, I was therefore compelled to resign my connection with the Society, which had hitherto supplied my salary.

My satisfaction was great when my friend and colleague Mr. Jones was led to take the same step; we were both profoundly thankful that the separation was friendly on both sides. Indeed, we had the joy of knowing that the step we took brought approval from several members of the Committee, although the Society as a whole could not come to our position. Depending upon God alone for supplies, we were able to continue a measure of connection with our former supporters, sending home journals, etc. for publication as before, as long as the Society continued to exist.

The step we had taken did try our faith. I was not at all sure what God would have me do or whether He would meet my need to enable me to continue working as before. I had no friends from whom I expected supplies. I did not know what means the Lord might use, but I was willing to give up all my time to the service of evangelization among the heathen, if He would supply the smallest amount on which I could live. If He was not pleased to do this, I was prepared to undertake whatever work might be necessary to supply myself, giving all the time that could be spared from such a calling to more distinctly missionary efforts. But God blessed and prospered me; how glad and thankful I felt when the separation was complete! I could look right up into my Father's face with a satisfied heart – ready, by His grace, to do the next thing as He might teach me and sure of His loving care.

And how blessedly He did lead me on and provide for me I can never, never tell. It was like a continuation of some of my earlier home experiences. My faith was not untried; it often, often failed, and I was sorry and ashamed of the failure to trust such a Father. But oh! I was learning to know Him. I would not even then have missed the trial. He became so near, so real, so intimate. The occasional difficulty about funds never came from an insufficient supply for personal needs, but as a result of ministering to the needs of scores of the hungry and dying ones around us. Other trials eclipsed these difficulties; greater trials brought forth richer fruits. How glad one is now, not only to know with dear Miss Havergal that:

> They who trust Him wholly
> Find Him wholly true,

but also when we fail to trust fully, He still remains unchangingly faithful. He *is* wholly true whether we trust or not. *If we believe not, yet he abideth faithful: he cannot deny himself.* But oh, how we dishonor our Lord whenever we fail to trust Him, and what peace, blessing, and triumph we lose in thus sinning against the Faithful One! May we never again presume to doubt Him in anything.

The year 1857 was a troublesome time and closed with the notorious bombardment of Canton by the British and the commencement of our second Chinese war. Rumors of trouble were everywhere, and in many places, the missionaries encountered danger. This was especially the case in Ningpo, and in answer to prayer, the preserving care of God was most evident. When the awful news of the bombardment of Canton reached the Cantonese in Ningpo, their wrath and indignation knew no bounds, and they immediately set to work to plot the destruction of all the foreign residents in the city and neighborhood. It was well known that many of the foreigners were in the habit of meeting for worship every Sunday evening at one of the missionary houses. They planned to surround the place on a given occasion and make short work of all those present, later cutting off any who might not be present.

The sanction of the Tao T'ai, or chief civil magistrate of the city, was obtained, and nothing remained to hinder the execution of the plot. The foreigners were, of course, entirely ignorant. (A similar plot against the Portuguese a few months later was carried out, and between fifty and sixty were massacred in open daylight.) It so happened, however, that one of those acquainted with the conspiracy had a friend engaged in the service of the missionaries. Being anxious for his safety, he was led to warn him of the coming danger and urge him to leave foreign employment. The servant made the matter known to his master, and thus the little community became aware of their peril. Realizing the gravity of the situation, they determined to meet together at the house of one of their number to seek the protection of the Most High and hide under the shadow of His wings. They did not meet in vain.

At the very time we were praying, the Lord was working. He led an inferior mandarin, the Superintendent of Customs, to call upon the Tao T'ai and challenge him concerning the wisdom of permitting such an attempt, which he assured him would rouse the foreigners in other places to come with armed forces to avenge the death of their countrymen and raze the city.

The Tao T'ai replied that, when the foreigners came for that purpose, he would deny all knowledge of or complicity in the plot. He would direct their vengeance against the Cantonese, who would in their turn be destroyed. "And thus," said he, "we shall get rid of both Cantonese and foreigners by one stroke of policy."

The Superintendent of Customs assured him that all such attempts at evasion would be useless. Finally, the Tao T'ai withdrew his permission from the Cantonese and prohibited the attack. This took place at the very time when we were asking protection of the Lord, though we did not discover the facts until some weeks later. Thus again we were led to prove that:

> Sufficient is Thine arm alone,
> And our defence is sure.

I cannot attempt to give any historical record of the events of this period, but before 1857 ended, Mr. Jones and I were cheered by tokens of blessing. It is interesting to recall the circumstances connected with the first profession of faith in Christ, which encouraged us.

On one occasion, I was preaching the good news of salvation through the finished work of Christ, when a middle-aged man stood up and testified before his assembled countrymen to his faith in the power of the gospel.

"I have long sought for the truth," said he earnestly, "as my fathers did before me; but I have never found it. I have traveled far and near, but without obtaining it. I have found no rest in Confucianism, Buddhism, or Taoism; but I do find rest in what I have heard here tonight. Henceforth, I am a believer in Jesus."

This man was one of the leading officers of a sect of reformed Buddhists in Ningpo. A short time after his confession of faith in the Savior, there was a meeting of the sect over which he had formerly presided. I accompanied him to that meeting, and there, to his former co-religionists, he testified of the peace he had obtained in believing. Soon after, one of his former companions was converted and baptized. Both now sleep in Jesus. The first of these two continued to preach to his countrymen the good news of great joy. A few nights after his conversion, he asked how long this gospel had been known in England. He was told that we had known it for hundreds of years.

"What!" said he, amazed. "Is it possible that for hundreds of years you have had the knowledge of this good news in your possession and have only now come to preach it to us? My father sought after the truth for more than twenty years and died without finding it. Oh, why did you not come sooner?"

A whole generation has passed away since that mournful inquiry was made; but how many, alas, might repeat the same question today? In the meantime, more than two hundred million have been swept into eternity without an offer of salvation. How long shall this continue, and the Master's words, *to every creature*, remain unheeded?

Students' quarters, Gan-k'ing Training Home

CHAPTER 16

Timely Supplies

Not infrequently, our God brings His people into difficulties on purpose, so they may come to know Him as they could not otherwise have done. Then He reveals Himself as *a very present help in trouble*, and makes the heart glad indeed at each fresh revelation of a Father's faithfulness. We who only see a small part of the sweet issues of trial often feel that we would not have wanted to miss them. How much more shall we bless and magnify His name when all the hidden things are brought to light!

In the autumn of 1857, one year after I settled in Ningpo, a little incident occurred that strengthened our faith in the lovingkindness and ever-watchful care of God.

A brother in the Lord, the Rev. John Quarterman of the American Presbyterian Mission North, was taken with virulent smallpox, and it was my mournful privilege to nurse him through his suffering illness to its fatal close. When all was over, I needed to lay aside the garments I wore for fear of transmitting the infection to others. Not having sufficient money in hand to purchase what was needful to make this change, I prayed. The Lord answered with the unexpected arrival of a long lost box of clothing from Swatow that had remained in the care of the Rev. William Burns when I left him for Shanghai in the early summer of the previous year. The arrival of those things at this juncture was as appropriate as it was remarkable, and brought a sweet sense of the Father's provision.

About two months later, the following was penned:

November 18th, 1857

Many seem to think that I am very poor. This certainly is true enough in one sense, but I thank God it is *as poor, yet making many rich; as having nothing, and yet possessing all things.* And my God shall supply *all* my need; to Him be all the glory. I would not, if I could, be otherwise than I am – entirely dependent upon the Lord and used as a channel of help to others.

On Saturday, our regular home mail arrived. As usual, that morning we supplied a breakfast to seventy of the destitute poor. Sometimes the number does not reach forty; at other times it exceeds eighty. They come to us every day except the Lord's Day, for then we cannot manage to attend to them and also get through all our other duties. Well, on that Saturday morning, we paid all expenses and provided ourselves for the next day, after which we had not a single dollar left between us. We did not know how the Lord was going to provide for Monday, but two scrolls in Chinese characters hung over our mantelpiece: "Ebenezer, Hitherto hath the Lord helped us"; and "Jehovah-Jireh, The Lord will provide," and He kept us from doubting for a moment. That very day the mail came, a week sooner than was expected, and Mr. Jones received a bill for two hundred and fourteen dollars. We thanked God and took courage. We took the bill to a merchant, and although there is usually a delay of several days in getting the change, this time he said, "Send down on Monday." We sent, and though he had not been able to exchange all the dollars, he let us have seventy on account. All was well. Oh, it is sweet to live totally dependent upon the Lord, who never fails us!

On Monday, the poor had their breakfast as usual, for we had not told them not to come. We were sure that this was the Lord's work, and the Lord would provide. We could not help our eyes filling with tears of gratitude when we saw not only our own needs supplied, but also the widow and the orphan, the blind and the lame, the friendless and the destitute, together provided for by the bounty of Him who feeds the ravens. *O magnify the LORD with me, and let us exalt his name together. . . . O taste and see that the LORD is good: blessed is the man that trusteth in him. O fear the LORD, ye His saints: for there is no want to them that fear him. The young lions do lack, and suffer hunger: but they that seek the LORD shall not want any good thing* – and if not good, why want it?

But even two hundred dollars cannot last forever, and by New Year's Day supplies were again getting low. At last, on January 6, 1858, only one solitary coin, the twentieth part of a penny, remained in the joint possession of Mr. Jones and me. Even though we were troubled, we looked to God once again to manifest His gracious care. We found enough provision in the house to supply a meager breakfast. After that, having neither food for the rest of the day nor money to buy any, we could only turn to Him who was able to supply all our need with the petition: *Give us this day our daily bread.*

After prayer and deliberation, we thought that perhaps we should dispose of something we possessed to meet our immediate needs. But on looking around, we saw nothing that we could spare and little that the Chinese would purchase for ready money. We might have had credit, if we could have conscientiously availed ourselves of it, but we believed this to be unscriptural as well as inconsistent with the position we were in. We had one article – an iron stove – which we knew the Chinese would readily purchase, but we regretted the necessity of parting with it. At length, however, we set out to the founder's. After a walk of some distance, we came to the river, which we had intended to cross by a floating bridge of boats, but here the Lord shut up our path. The bridge had been carried away during the preceding night, and the river was only passable by means of a ferry, the fare for which was two coins for each person. As we only possessed one coin, clearly our path was to return and await God's own intervention on our behalf.

Upon reaching home, we found that Mrs. Jones had gone with the children to dine at a friend's house, in response to an invitation she accepted some days previously. Mr. Jones, though himself included in the invitation, refused to go and leave me to fast alone. So we set to work and carefully searched the cupboards. Though there was nothing to eat, we found a small packet of cocoa, which, with a little hot water, somewhat revived us. After this, we again cried to the Lord in our trouble, and the Lord heard and saved us out of all our distresses. For while we were still upon our knees, a letter arrived from England containing a remittance.

This timely supply met the immediate and urgent need of the day. We had the assured confidence that God, whose we were and whom we served, would not put to shame those whose whole and only trust was in Him.

My marriage had been arranged to take place just fourteen days after this date. And this expectation was not disappointed, *For the mountains shall depart, and the hills be removed; but my kindness shall not depart from thee, neither shall the covenant of my peace be removed.* Although during subsequent years our faith was often exercised, sometimes severely, He always proved faithful to His promise and never allowed us to lack any good thing.

Never, perhaps, was there a union that more fully realized the blessed truth: *Whoso findeth a wife findeth a good thing, and obtaineth favour of the LORD.* My dear wife was not only a precious gift to me, but God blessed many others through her during the twelve eventful years through which she was spared to those that loved her and to China.

Hers had been a life connection with missionary work in that great empire, for her father, the loved and devoted Samuel

Dyer, was among the very earliest representatives of the London Mission in the East. He reached the Straits as early as 1827, and for sixteen years he labored among the Chinese in Penang and Singapore, completing at the same time a valuable font of Chinese metallic type, the first of the kind that had then been attempted. Dying in 1843, it was never Mr. Dyer's privilege to realize his hopes of being able to settle on Chinese soil, but his children lived to see the country opened to the gospel and to take part in the great work that had been so dear to his heart. At the time of our marriage, my dear wife had been already living in Ningpo for several years with her friend Miss Aldersey, in whose missionary operations she was well qualified to render valuable assistance.

CHAPTER 17

God – A Refuge for Us

A somewhat different though not less manifest answer to prayer was granted early in the year 1859. My dear wife was brought very low by illness, and all hope of recovery seemed gone. Every remedy had proved futile, and Dr. Parker, who attended her, had nothing more to suggest. Life was ebbing away. The only hope was that God might yet see fit to raise her up in answer to believing but submissive prayer.

On the afternoon of the usual prayer meeting among the missionaries, I sent a request for prayer, which was most warmly received. Just at this time, a remedy that had not yet been tried came to my mind, and I felt that I must hasten to consult Dr. Parker as to the possibility of using it. It was a moment of anguish. The hollow temples, sunken eyes, and pinched features denoted the nearness of death. It seemed more than questionable as to whether her life would hold out until my return. It was nearly two miles to Dr. Parker's house, and every moment appeared long. On my way, while wrestling mightily with God in prayer, the precious words were brought to my soul with power: *And call upon me in the day of trouble: I will deliver thee, and thou shall glorify me.* I was at once able to plead in faith, and the result was deep, deep, unspeakable peace and joy. All consciousness of distance was gone. Dr. Parker cordially approved of my suggestion, but upon arriving at home, I saw at a glance that the desired change had taken place in the absence of this or any other remedy. The pinched appearance of her face had given place to the calmness of tranquil slumber, and not one symptom remained to retard recovery to health and strength.

Being spared the loss of my own loved one, it was with added sympathy and sorrow that I felt for Dr. Parker, when in the autumn of the same year, his own wife very suddenly died. Because the doctor needed to return at once with his motherless children to Glasgow, temporary arrangements were made for the management of the Mission Hospital in Ningpo, for he alone had been responsible. Under these circumstances, he requested that I take up the work, at least so far as the dispensary was concerned. After waiting upon the Lord for guidance, I felt led to undertake not only the dispensary, but also that of the hospital, relying solely upon the faithfulness of a prayer-hearing God to furnish the means required for its support.

The funds for the maintenance of the hospital had been supplied by the proceeds of the doctor's foreign medical practice; with his departure, these ceased. But had God not said that whatever we ask in the name of the Lord Jesus shall be done? And are we not told to seek first the kingdom of God, not the means to advance it, and all these things shall be added to us? Such promises were surely sufficient. Eight days before entering upon this responsibility, I did not have the remotest idea of ever doing this; friends at home could not have anticipated it either. But the Lord had foreseen the need, and already funds were on the way to supply it.

At times there were not less than fifty inpatients in the hospital, plus a large number who daily attended the outpatient department. Thirty beds were ordinarily allotted to free patients and their attendants and about as many to opium smokers, who paid for their board while being cured of the habit. As all the wants of the sick in the wards were free, in addition to the needs for the outpatient work, the daily expenses were considerable.

Also, a number of native attendants were required, which involved their support.

When Dr. Parker handed the hospital over to me, he was able to leave money that would meet the salaries and working expenses of the current month but little more. Being unable to guarantee their support, his native staff retired. I mentioned the circumstances to the members of our little church, and some volunteered to help me, depending upon the Lord. They continued to wait upon God with me that in some way or other He would provide for His own work. Day by day, the stores diminished, and they were all but exhausted when a remarkable letter reached me from a friend in England, which contained a check for fifty pounds. The letter stated that the sender had recently lost his father and had inherited his property. Not desiring to increase his personal spending, he wished to hold the money, which had been left to him, to further the Lord's work. He enclosed the fifty pounds, saying that I might know of some special need for it. He left me free to use it for my own support or in any way that the Lord might lead me, only asking to know how it was applied and whether there was need for more.

After a little season of thanksgiving with my dear wife, I called my native helpers into our little chapel and translated the letter to them. I do not need to say how they rejoiced and that we together praised God. They returned to their work in the hospital with overflowing hearts and told the patients what a great God was ours, appealing to them as to whether their idols had ever helped them so. Both helpers and patients were blessed spiritually through this remarkable provision, and from that time the Lord provided all that was necessary for carrying on the hospital, in addition to what we needed for the maintenance of my own family and sustaining other branches of missionary work under my care. Nine months later, when I was obliged to relinquish this charge due to failure in my health, I was able to leave more funds in hand for the support of the hospital than were available at the time I undertook it.

Not only were monetary supplies granted in answer to prayer, but many lives were spared. People in apparently hopeless stages of disease were restored, and cases of serious and dangerous operations were successful. In the case of one poor man, whose legs were amputated under very unfavorable circumstances, recovery took place with such rapidity that both wounds were healed in less than two weeks. And more permanent benefits than these were conferred. Many were convinced of the truth of Christianity; more than a few sought the Lord in faith and prayer and experienced the power of the Great Physician to cure the sin-sick soul. During the nine months I oversaw the work, sixteen patients from the hospital were baptized, and more than thirty others became candidates for admission into one or another of the Christian churches in the city.

Thus the year 1860 began with many openings, but time and strength were too limited to make use of them to the best advantage. For some time the help of additional workers had been a much-felt need. In January, definite prayer was made to the Lord of the harvest that He would send more laborers into this special portion of the great world's field. Writing to relatives at home in England under the date of January 16, 1860, I thus expressed the deep longing of our hearts:

> Do you know any earnest, devoted young men, desirous of serving God in China who, not wishing for more than their actual support, would be willing to come and labor here? Oh, for four or five such helpers! They would probably begin to preach in Chinese in six months' time. In answer to prayer, the necessary means for their support would be found.

But no one came to help us, and under the incessant physical and mental strain involved in the care of the hospital during Dr. Parker's absence, as well as the continued discharge of my other missionary duties, my own health began to fail rapidly. It became a serious question as to whether it would be necessary to return to England for a time.

It was hard to face this possibility. The growing church and work seemed to need our presence, and it was no small trial to part from those we had learned to love in the Lord. Thirty or forty native Christians had been gathered into the recently organized church, and the crowded meetings and warm-hearted earnestness of the converts spoke of a future of much promise. At last, however, completely prostrated by repeated attacks of illness, the only hope of restoration seemed to lie in a voyage to England and a brief stay in its more favorable climate. This necessity, though painful at the time, proved to be only another opportunity for the manifestation of the faithfulness and loving care of Him *who worketh all things after the counsel of his own will.*

As before, the Lord was present with His aid. The means for our journey were supplied so liberally that we were able to bring with us a native Christian to assist in translation or other literary work and instruct helpers in the language, those whom the Lord might raise up for the extension of the Mission. We had no doubt He would give us fellow laborers, for we had been enabled to seek them from Him in earnest and believing prayer for many months.

The day before leaving China, we wrote to our friend W. T. Berger Esq., whom we had known in England and who had always strengthened our hands in the Lord while in that distant land: "We are bringing with us a young Chinese brother to assist in literary work, and I hope also in teaching the dialect to those whom the Lord may induce to return with us."

And throughout the voyage, our earnest cry to God was that He would overrule our stay at home for good to China and make it instrumental in raising up at least five helpers to labor in the province of Cheh-kiang.

The way in which it pleased the Lord to answer these earnest and believing prayers and how *exceeding abundantly* He crowned them, we shall now sketch in brief outline.

CHAPTER 18

A New Agency Needed

F or my thoughts are not your thoughts, neither are your ways my ways, saith the LORD. For as the heavens are higher than the earth, so are my ways higher than your ways, and my thoughts than your thoughts (Isaiah 55:8-9). How true are these words! When the Lord is bringing in great blessing in the best possible way, how often our unbelieving hearts are feeling, if not saying, like Jacob of old: *all these things are against me.* Or we are filled with fear, as the disciples were when the Lord, walking on the waters, drew near to quiet the troubled sea and bring them to their desired haven. And yet, mere common sense ought to tell us that He, whose way is perfect, *can* make no mistakes. He who has promised to *perfect that which concerneth* us, whose care counts the very hairs of our head and forms our circumstances, *must* know better than we the way to advance our interests and to glorify His name.

> Blind unbelief is *sure* to err
>   And scan His work in vain;
> God is His own Interpreter,
>   And He will make it plain.

It seemed a great calamity to me that failure of health compelled me to relinquish work for God in China, just when it was more fruitful than ever before. To leave the little band of Christians in Ningpo, needing much care and teaching, was a great sorrow. The sorrow was not lessened when, on reaching

England, medical reports assured me that returning to China was impossible for years to come. Little did I realize that the long separation from China was a necessary step towards the formation of a work that God would bless as He has blessed the China Inland Mission. While in the field, the pressure of the immediate was so great that I could not think much of the still-greater needs of the regions farther inland. If they were thought of, I could do nothing for them. But while detained for some years in England, daily viewing the whole country on the large map on the wall of my study, I was as near to the vast regions of Inland China as to the smaller districts in which I had labored personally for God. Prayer was often the only resource by which the burdened heart could gain any relief.

As a long absence from China appeared inevitable, the next question was how best to serve China while in England. This led to my engaging with the late Rev. F. F. Gough of the Church Missionary Society for several years in the revision of a version of the New Testament into the colloquial language of Ningpo for the British and Foreign Bible Society. In my shortsightedness, I saw no use in this undertaking than that the book, and the marginal references, would be of use to the native Christians. But I have seen since that, without those months of feeding and feasting on the Word of God, I would have been quite unprepared to form a mission like the China Inland Mission.

In the study of that divine Word, I learned that, rather than elaborate pleas for help to obtain successful laborers, what was needed was, first, earnest prayer to God to provide laborers, and second, the deepening of the spiritual life of the church so men would be unable to stay at home. I saw that the apostolic plan was not to raise ways and means, but to go and do the work, trusting in His sure Word who has said, *But seek ye first the kingdom of God and his righteousness, and all these things shall be added unto you.*

In the meantime, the prayer for workers for Cheh-kiang was being answered. The first, Mr. Meadows, sailed for China with his young wife in January 1862 through the kind cooperation and aid of our friend Mr. Berger. The second left England in 1864, having her passage provided by the Foreign Evangelization Society. The third and fourth reached Ningpo on July 24, 1865. A fifth soon followed them, reaching Ningpo in September 1865. Thus, the prayer for the five workers was answered, and we were encouraged to look to God for still greater things.

Months of earnest prayer with more than a few abortive efforts had resulted in a deep conviction that a special agency was essential for the evangelization of Inland China. At this time, I had not only the daily help of prayer and conference with my beloved friend and fellow worker the late Rev. F. F. Gough, but also invaluable aid and counsel from Mr. and Mrs. Berger, with whom my dear wife (whose judgment and piety were priceless at this juncture) and I spent many days in prayerful deliberation. The grave possibility of interfering with existing missionary operations at home was foreseen, but it was concluded that by simple trust in God, a suitable agency could be formed and sustained without causing injury to any existing work. I had a growing conviction that God would have *me* to seek from Him the needed workers and to go forth with them. But for a long time, unbelief hindered my taking the first step.

How inconsistent unbelief always is! I had no doubt that, if I prayed for workers, "*in* the name" of the Lord Jesus Christ, they would be given me. I had no doubt that, in answer to such prayer, the means for our advancing would be provided, and doors would be opened before us in unreached parts of the empire. But I had not learned to trust God for "keeping" power and grace for myself, so no wonder that I could not trust Him to keep others who might be prepared to go with me. I feared that in the midst of the dangers, difficulties, and trials, which would be connected with such a work, some who were inexperienced Christians might break down. They could bitterly reproach me for having encouraged them to undertake an enterprise for which they were not prepared.

Yet, what was I to do? The feeling of blood guiltiness became more and more intense. Simply because I refused to ask for them, the laborers did not come forward, did not go out to China, and every day tens of thousands were passing away to Christless graves! Perishing China filled my heart and mind until there was no rest by day and little sleep by night, causing my health to break down. At the invitation of my beloved and honored friend Mr. George Pearse (of the stock exchange), I went to spend a few days with him in Brighton.

On Sunday, June 25, 1865, unable to bear the sight of a congregation of a thousand Christian people rejoicing in their own security while millions were perishing for lack of knowledge, I wandered out on the sands alone in great spiritual agony. The Lord conquered my unbelief there, and I surrendered myself to God for this service. I told Him that all the responsibility as to issues and consequences must rest with Him. As His servant, my responsibility was to obey and to follow Him – His was to direct, care for, and guide us. Need I say that peace at once flowed into my burdened heart? There and then, I asked Him for twenty-four fellow workers, two for each of the eleven Inland provinces, which were without a missionary, and two for Mongolia. Writing the petition in the margin of the Bible I had with me, I returned home with a heart enjoying rest that it had been a stranger to for months and with an assurance that the Lord would bless His own work and I would share in the blessing. I had previously prayed and asked for prayer that workers might be raised up for the eleven then-unoccupied provinces, but I had not surrendered myself to be their leader.

With the help of my dear wife, I wrote the little book *China's*

Spiritual Need and Claims. Every paragraph was steeped in prayer. With the help of Mr. Berger, who gave valuable aid in the revision of the manuscript and bore the expense of printing an edition of three thousand copies, it was soon put in circulation. As opportunity permitted, I spoke publicly of the proposed work, especially at the Perth and Mildmay conferences of 1865, and continued in prayer for fellow workers, who were soon raised up. After due correspondence, they were invited to my home in East London. When one house became insufficient, and the occupant of the adjoining house moved, I was able to rent it. When that became insufficient, further accommodation was provided close by. Soon there were a number of men and women doing preparatory training and engaging in evangelistic work, which tested in some measure their qualifications as soul winners.

CHAPTER 19

The Formation of the CIM

In the year 1865, the China Inland Mission (CIM) was organized, and the workers already in the field were incorporated into it. Our friend W. T. Berger Esq., residing at Saint Hill near East Grinstead, undertook the direction of the home department of the work during my anticipated absence in China. I could not have gone forward without his help and encouragement. As soon as arrangements could be completed, I proposed to go with the volunteers and take the direction of the work in the field. Our friends at home were sending unsolicited contributions from time to time for the support of the workers already in China, and every need was met.

Now, however, we needed to plan for a party of sixteen or seventeen to go out, and estimated that from fifteen hundred to two thousand pounds might be required to cover outfits, passage money, and initial expenses. I wrote a little pamphlet, *Occasional Paper, No. 1*, intending to give donors and friends accounts of our work in China in successive numbers. In that paper, I stated the anticipated needs for floating the enterprise. I expected that God would incline the hearts of some of the readers to send contributions; I had determined never to use personal solicitation, make collections, or issue collecting books. Missionary boxes were not objectionable, and we had a few prepared for those who might ask for them and have continued to use them ever since.

It was February 6, 1866, when I sent my manuscript of *Occasional Paper, No. 1* with a design for the cover to the printer. From delays in engraving and printing, it was March 12 when the bales of pamphlets were delivered at my house. Now on February 6, a daily prayer meeting from noon to one o'clock had begun to ask for the needed funds. And we did not ask in vain, as the following excerpt from *Occasional Paper, No. 2* will show:

The receipts for 1864 were £51:14s.; for 1865, from January to June, £221:12:6, plus two free passages; from June to December, £923:12:8. Hindrances having occurred, the manuscript of *Occasional Paper, No. 1* was not completed until February 6, 1866. Up to this time, we had received (from December 30) £170:8:3.

We felt encouraged by the receipt of so much money in little more than a month, as it was unsolicited by us – except from God. But it was also evident that we needed to ask the Lord to do even greater things for us, or it would be impossible for a party of ten to sixteen to leave in the middle of May. Daily united prayer was therefore offered to God for the funds needed for the outfits and passages of all He would have go out in May.

Due to the delays in the printing of the *Occasional Paper, No. 1*, it was not ready for the publisher until March 12. On this day, I again examined my mission cashbook, and the comparison of the result of the two similar periods of one month and six days each, one before and one after special prayer for £1500 to £2000, was very striking:

Receipts from Dec. 30th to Feb. 6th	£170	8	3			
Feb. 6th to Mar. 12th	£1774	5	11			
Funds advised, since received	200	0	0			
			—————	£1974	5	11

This, it will be noticed, was prior to the circulation of the *Occasional Paper*, and, consequently, was not the result of it. It was God's faithful response to the united prayers of those He had called to serve Him in the gospel of His dear Son.

We can now compare these two periods with a third of the same length. From March 12 to April 18, the receipts were £529, showing that when God had supplied the special need, the special supply also ceased. Truly there is a living God, and He is the hearer and answerer of prayer.

But this gracious answer to prayer made it a little difficult to circulate *Occasional Paper, No. 1*, for it stated as a need that which was already supplied. The difficulty was made worse by the inclusion of a colored inset stating that the funds for outfit and passage were already in hand in answer to prayer. We were reminded of the difficulty of Moses – not a very common one in the present day – and of the proclamation he had to send through the camp to the people to prepare no more for the building of the tabernacle, as the gifts in hand were already too much. We are convinced that if there were less solicitation for money and more dependence upon the power of the Holy Ghost and the deepening of spiritual life, the experience of Moses would be a common one in every branch of Christian work.

Preparations for sailing to China were at once taken up. About this time, I was asked to give a lecture on China in a village not very far from London, and I agreed on condition that there should be no collection and this should be announced on the posters. The gentleman who invited me and who kindly presided as chairman said he had never had that condition imposed before. He accepted it, however, and the posters were issued accordingly for the second or third of May. With the aid of a large map, the extent and population and deep spiritual need of China was presented, and many were evidently impressed.

At the close of the meeting, the chairman said that by my request it had been announced on the posters that there would be no collection, but he felt that many present would be distressed and burdened if they did not have the opportunity of contributing to the proposed good work. He trusted that since the proposition originated entirely from him and expressed, he felt sure, the feelings of many in the audience, I should not object to it. I begged, however, that the condition agreed to might be carried out. I pointed out, among other reasons for making no collection, that the very reason cited by our kind chairman was, to my mind, one of the strongest for not making it. My wish was that each one should go home burdened with the deep need of China and ask God what He would have them do, not that those present should be relieved by making a contribution that might there and then be convenient under the influence of a present emotion. If, after thought and prayer, they were satisfied that a monetary contribution was what He wanted of them, it could be given to any Missionary Society having agents in China, or it might be posted to our London office. In many cases God might not want a money contribution, but rather personal consecration to His service abroad or the giving up of a son or daughter – more precious than silver or gold – to His service. I added that I thought the tendency of a collection was to leave the impression that the all-important thing was *money*, but no amount of money could convert a single soul. What was needed were men and women filled with the Holy Ghost to give themselves to the work, for the support of such would never be lacking. As my wish was evidently very strong, the chairman kindly yielded to it and closed the meeting. He told me, however, at the supper table that he thought it was a mistake on my part, and in spite of all I had said, a few persons had put some little contributions into his hands.

Next morning at breakfast, my kind host came in a little late and acknowledged not having had a very good night. After breakfast, he asked me to his study and gave me the contributions handed to him the night before. He said, "I thought last night, Mr. Taylor, that you were wrong about a collection; I am now convinced you were quite right. As I thought in the night of that stream of souls in China ever passing onward into the dark, I could only cry as you suggested, 'Lord, what wilt Thou have *me* to do?' I think I have obtained the guidance I sought, and here it is." He handed me a check for five hundred pounds, adding that if there had been a collection, he would have given a few pounds, but now this check was the result of having spent no small part of the night in prayer.

I need scarcely say how surprised and thankful I was for this gift. At the breakfast table, I had received a letter from shipping agents Killick, Martin & Company, in which they stated that they could offer us the whole passenger accommodation of the ship *Lammermuir*. I went directly to the ship, found it in every way suitable, and paid the check on the account. As stated before, the necessary funds had already been in hand for some time, but the coincidence of the simultaneous offer of the ship accommodation and this munificent gift – God's *exceeding abundantly* – greatly encouraged my heart.

On the twenty-sixth of May, we sailed for China in the *Lammermuir*, a missionary party of sixteen, plus my four children, their nurse, and Miss Bausum, later Mrs. Barchet, in all, twenty-two passengers. Mr. Berger took charge of the home department, and thus the CIM was fully inaugurated.

CHAPTER 20

The Mission in 1894

The events sketched in the last two chapters have been more fully delineated by Miss Guinness in her interesting *Story Of The China Inland Mission*, which continues its history to the present date. It is indeed a record of the goodness of God, every remembrance of which calls for gratitude and praise. Here we can only briefly mention a few facts, referring our readers to Miss Guinness's work for all details.

After a voyage of many mercies, the *Lammermuir* party safely reached China. During the first ten years, stations and out-stations were opened in many cities and towns in four provinces, which had been unreached by the gospel previously. At home, Mr. and Mrs. Berger continued their devoted service until March 19, 1872; I had returned to England the year before. Shortly after this, the London Council was formed, which has been assisted by an auxiliary Council of ladies for several years. A Scotch Council was also formed in Glasgow a few years ago.

A visit to America in 1888 resulted in the formation of the Council for North America, and a similar Council for Australia was begun in Melbourne two years later. In the field, a China Council was organized in 1886, composed of senior missionaries who meet quarterly in Shanghai.

Closely associated with the CIM are seven Committees – in England, Norway, Sweden (two), Finland, Germany, and the United States – which send out and support their own missionaries, who have the assistance of the educational and other advantages of the CIM in China, and who work under its direction.

The staff of the Mission in May 1893 consisted of 552 missionaries (including wives and associates). There were also 326 native helpers (95 of whom were unpaid) working as pastors, evangelists, teachers, book peddlers, and Bible women in fourteen different provinces.

Qualified candidates for missionary labor are accepted without restriction as to denomination, provided they are sound in the faith in all fundamental truths. These individuals go out depending upon God for temporal supplies with the clear understanding that the officers of the Mission do not guarantee any income whatsoever. They know that as they will not go into debt, they can only minister to the extent that the funds sent from time to time will allow. But we praise God that during the past twenty-eight years, such ministry has always been possible. Our God has supplied all our need and has withheld no good thing.

All the expenses of the Mission at home and abroad are met by voluntary contributions, sent to the offices of the Mission without personal solicitation by those who wish to aid in this effort to spread the knowledge of the gospel throughout China. The income for the year 1892 was about thirty-four thousand pounds from all sources – Great Britain, the continent of Europe, North America, Australia, and China.

Some of the missionaries who have private property have gone out at their own expense and do not take anything from the Mission funds.

Stations have been opened in ten of the eleven provinces, which were previously without Protestant missionaries. However, we have had to retire from one of these. The eleventh province has been visited several times, and it is hoped that a permanent work may soon begin in it.

More than two hundred stations and out-stations have been opened in fourteen of the eighteen provinces, where either missionaries or native laborers are resident. Over six thousand converts have been baptized from the beginning, four thousand of whom are now living and in fellowship.

The Mission in 1902

The year 1894, in which the first edition of *A Retrospect* appeared, was marked by the erection of large and commodious premises for the work of the Mission. Early in the following year, the houses in Pyrland Road, which had so long formed the home of the Mission in England, were vacated, and Newington Green, London, N., became the address of the Mission offices and home.

From that date until the Boxer Rebellion of 1900, the Mission made steady progress. The development of the work in China was accompanied by corresponding developments in the home departments of the Mission in England, America, and Australia.

In January 1900, before the Boxer Rebellion, there were in connection with the Mission 811 missionaries, including wives and associates, 171 stations, 223 out-stations, 387 chapels, 581 paid native helpers, 193 unpaid native helpers, 8,557 communicants in fellowship, and 12,964 baptized from the commencement. There were 266 organized churches, 788 boarding scholars, 1,382 day scholars, 6 hospitals, 18 dispensaries, and 46 opium refuges.

During the terrible year of 1900, when no fewer than 135 missionaries, 53 missionaries' children, and many thousands of Chinese Christians were cruelly murdered, the China Inland Mission lost 58 missionaries and 21 children. The records of these unparalleled times of suffering have been told in *Martyred Missionaries Of The China Inland Mission* and *Last Letters*, books that will be found advertised at the end of this volume. Apart from loss of life, there was an immense amount of Mission property destroyed, and the missionaries were compelled to retire from their stations in most parts of China.

The doors closed by this rebellion have all been reopened by the goodness of God. In those districts that suffered most from the massacres, the work has largely been one of reorganization. But throughout China generally, there has been a spirit of awakening and a time of enlarged opportunity, which is a loud call for more men and women to volunteer to step into the gaps and fill the places of those who have fallen.

Among recent developments, we would especially mention the opening of a new home center in Philadelphia, in the USA. The total income of the Mission for 1901 was £53,633 = $257,712, and the total received in England alone for 1902 was £51,446 = $246,912. The total membership of the Mission in June 1902 was 761.

Current information about the progress of the work in China may be obtained from *China's Millions*, the mouthpiece of the Mission. It is published monthly and may be ordered through any bookseller from Morgan & Scott, 12 Paternoster Buildings E.C., for 1s. per year, or direct by post from the offices of the Mission, Newington Green, London, N., for 1s. 6d. per annum.

The Australian edition of *China's Millions* may be ordered at the same price from M. L. Hutchinson, Little Collins Street, or from the Mission offices, 267 Collins Street, Melbourne. The North American edition will be sent post-free from the Mission offices, 507 Church Street, Toronto, Canada, for fifty cents per annum.

Prayer meetings on behalf of the work in China are held at the principal home centers of the Mission as follows: every Saturday afternoon from four to six o'clock at Newington Green, London; every Friday evening at eight o'clock at 507 Church Street, Toronto; and every Saturday afternoon at four o'clock in the office, 267 Collins Street, Melbourne. A hearty invitation to attend any one of these meetings is given to anyone residing in or visiting any of these cities.

MAP OF CHINA

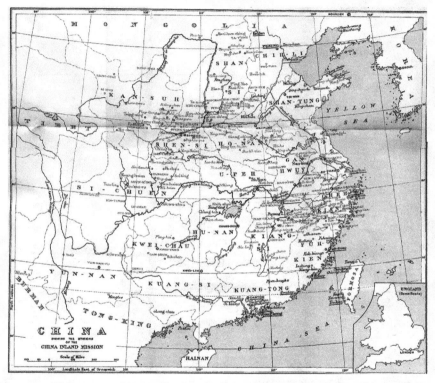

1. All Protestant Mission Stations in China up to June 1866, when the CIM was founded (they numbered fifteen) These are underlined in black.

2. The Stations of the China Inland Mission which (with the exception of Ningpo and Fung-hwa) have been opened since June 1866. These are printed in red.

STATIONS OF THE CHINA INLAND MISSION
1900
(BEFORE THE BOXER REBELLION)

The best guide to the stations of the Mission is the new China Inland Mission Map (size 44 x 38 inches, mounted on linen, colored, varnished, and hung on rollers), price 8s. *net*, carriage and packing extra. Mounted to fold, 8s. *net*, post-free.

Provinces.	Stations.	Work Begun.
Kan-suh, 1876	Liang-chau	1888
	Si-ning	1885
	Lan-Chau	1885
	Ts'ing Chau	1878
Area, 125,450 square miles	Fu K'ing	1899
Population, 9,285,377	P'ing-liang	1895
	King-chau	1895
	Ts'ing-ning	1897
	Chen Yuen	1897
	Tong-chi	1899
Shen-si, 1876	Lung-chau	1893
	Feng-tsiang	1888
	Mei-hien	1893
	K'ien-chau	1894
Area, 67,400 square miles	Chau-chih	1893
Population, 8,432,193	Sang-kia-chuang	1894
	Hing-p'ing	1893
	Si-Gan	1893
	Ying-kia-wei	1893
	Chen-kia-hu	1897
	Lan-t'ien	1895

	K'ien-yang	1897
	Wu-ch'ang	1897
	Sanshui	1897
	Tung Chau	1891
	Han-ch'eng	1897
	Han-chung	1879
	Ch'eng-ku	1887
	Si-hsiang	1896
	Yang-hien	1896
	Hing-an	1898
Shan-si, 1876	Ta t'ung	1886
	Hwen-yuen	1898
	Soh-p'ing	1895
	Tsö-yuin	1895
	Ying-chau	1897
	Hiao-i	1887
	Kiai-hiu	1891
	Ma Sih Chau	1885
	Ta-ning	1885
	Kih-chau	1891
	Tsin Ho	1893
	Pingyao	1888
Area, 56,268 square miles	Hoh-chau	1886
Population, 12,211,453	Hung-t'ung	1886
	Yoh-yang	1896
	P'ing-yang	1879
	K'üh-wu	1885
	I-shï	1891
	Yüin-ch'eng	1888
	Mei-ti-kiai	1895
	Hiai-chau	1895

	Lu-ch'eng	1889
	Ü-wu	1896
	Luan	1889
	Kiang-chau	1898

Chih-li, 1887	Tien-tsin	1888
Area, 58,949 square miles	Pao-t'ing	1891
Population, 17,937,000	Hwuy-luh	1887
	Shun Teh	1888

Shan-tung, 1879	Chefoo	1879
	"Sanatorium"	1880
	"Boys' School"	1880
Area, 53,762 square miles	"Girls'	1884
Population, 36,247,835	"Preparatory School"	1895
	T'ung Shin	1889
	Ninghai	1886

Ho-nan, 1875	Siang-ch'eng	1891
	Chau-kia-k'eo	1884
	Ho-nan	...
	Hopeh	...
	Ho-si	...
Area, 66,913 square miles	Cheung Chau	1895
Population, 22,115,827	Taikang	1895
	She-k'i-tien	1886
	Kwang-Chou-Wan	1899
	Hainan	1899
	King-tsï-kuan	1896

W. Si-ch'uan, 1877	Kwan-hien	1889
	Ch'eng-tu	1881

	Kia-ting	1888
Area of whole province,	Sui-fu	1888
166,800 square miles	Lu-chau	1890
	Hiao-shï	1899
	Ch'ung-k'ing	1877
	Ta-chien-lu	1897
E. Si-ch'uan, 1886	Kwang-yuen	1889
	Sin-tien-tsï	1892
	Pao-ning	1886
	Yingshan	1898
Population of whole	Kü-hien	1898
province, 67,712,897	Shun-k'ing	1896
	Pa-chau	1887
	Sui-ting	1899
	Wan-hien	1888
Hu-Peh, 1874	Lao-ho-k'ou	1887
Area, 70,450 square miles	Hankou	1889
Population, 34,244,685	I-ch'ang	1895
Gan-hwuy, 1869	T'ai-ho	1892
	Vinh Chau	1897
	Ch'eng-yang-kwan	1887
	Ku-Cheng	1887
	Fuh-hing-tsih (Lai-gan)	1898
	Loh Gan	1890
	Gan-k'ing	1869
Area, 48,461 square miles	Training Home	...
Population, 20,596,288	Wuhu	1893
	Kien Ping	1894
	Ning-kwoh	1874

	Kwang-teh	1890
	Ch'i-chau	1889
	Kien-teh	1892
	Hwuy-chau	1884
Kiang-su, 1854	Gan-tung	1891
	Ts'ing-kiang-pu	1869
	Kao Yiu	1888
	Yangzhou	1868
	Training Home	...
	Chinkiang	1888
Area, 44,500 square miles	Shanghai	1854
Population, 20,905,171	Financial Department	...
	Business Department	...
	Home	...
	Hospital	...
	Evangelistic Work	...
	Literary Work	...
Yun-nan, 1877	Bhamo (Upper Burma)	1875
Area, 107,969 square miles	Ta-li	1881
Population, 11,721,576	Yun-nan	1882
	K'üh-ts'ing	1889
Kwei-chau, 1877	Kwei-Yang	1877
	Gan-shun	1888
Area, 64,554 square miles	Tuh Shan	1893
Population, 7,669,181	Hing-i	1891
	(Work among Aborigines)	...
	Pang-hai	1897

Hu-nan, 1875	Ch'ang-teh	1898
Area, 74,320 square miles	Shenzhen	1898
Population, 21,002,604	Ch'a-ling	1898
Kiang-si, 1869	Kiu-kiang	1889
	Ku-ling Sanatorium	1898
	Ta-Ku-Tang	1873
	Nan-k'ang	1887
	Gan-ren	1889
	Rao-chau	1898
	Pekan	1893
	Kwei-k'i	1878
	Shang-ts'ing	1893
	Hü-wan	1899
	Ih-yang	1890
Area, 72,176 square miles	Ho-k'eo	1878
Population, 24,534,118	Yang-k'eo	1890
	Kwang-feng	1889
	Yuh-shan	1877
	Changshu	1895
	Kui-gan	1891
	Feng-kang	1891
	Kan-chau	1899
	Sin-feng	1899
	Lin-kiang	1898
	Nanchang	1898
	Uen-chau (*Itinerating*)	...
	Yung-sin	1899
Cheh-kiang, 1857	Hangzhou	1866
	Shaoxing	1866
	Sin-ch'ang	1870

	Kiu Tsui Chau	1872
	Ch'ang-shan	1878
	Lan-k'i	1894
Area, 39,150 square miles	Kin Hwa	1875
Population, 11,588,692	Yongkang	1882
	Tseh-k'i	1897
	Ch'u-chau	1875
	Lung Chuen	1894
	Uin-ho	1895
	Song Yang	1896
	Siao-mei	1896
	Tsin-yuan	1898
	Ningpo	1857
	Fenghua	1866
	Ninghai	1868
	T'ien-t'ai	1898
	T'ai-chau	1867
	Ling He District	...
	Hwang-yen	1896
	Tai Ping	1898
	Wun-chau	1867
	Bing-yae	1874

Printed by R. & R. Clark Ltd., *Edinburgh.*

About the Author

J. Hudson Taylor's father was deeply stirred about the spiritual state of China, and though he was an earnest and successful evangelist at home, his circumstances prevented him from ever going to China. But he was led to pray that if God should give him a son, he might be called and privileged to labor in the vast, needy empire. That prayer was answered when at 21 years of age, J. Hudson Taylor boarded a ship to China. Today, he's remembered as a pioneer to modern missions, and his initial mission is still going strong, more than 150 years after it began.

The hearty thanks of the Mission for the use of photographs and sketches are hereby tendered to the Rev. George Hayes for Nos. 4 and 6; Dr. G. Whitfield Guinness for Nos. 8, 12, 16, 25, and 28; Miss Davies for No. 23; Mr. Thomas Selkirk for Nos. 18 and 21; Mr. J. T. Reid for Nos. 14, 15, and 27; Mr. J. S. Rough for No. 30; Mr. Grainger for No. 19; Mr. E. Murray for No. 13; and also to other friends unknown by name.

In its early years, Duluth was a gold mine for lumber barons. Men were employed as lumberjacks and worked like beasts, only to be tossed aside like used equipment when no longer needed. The grand forests were raped for their prime timber, the balance burned wastefully. The men were coarse and hard, but they had to be to survive. More than any other people that ever lived in our land, these old-time lumberjacks could truthfully say, "No man cared for my soul."

That is, until God sent three men to the great Northwoods of our country – Frank Higgins, John Sornberger, and Al Channer. These men blazed new trails of the Spirit and founded an empire for God. They reached a sector of humanity for which no spiritual work had ever been done before, storming the Northwoods with a consuming passion for Christ. And with that passion, they also brought a heart as big as all outdoors, a love for men that burned like a flame, and a desperate desire to see these men saved.

Available where books are sold

CPSIA information can be obtained
at www.ICGtesting.com
Printed in the USA
BVHW030211230221
600876BV00010B/175